Source Code Analytics With Roslyn and JavaScript Data Visualization

Sudipta Mukherjee

Foreword by Dr. Darius Blasband

Apress®

Source Code Analytics With Roslyn and JavaScript Data Visualization

Sudipta Mukherjee
Varthur Hobli, India

ISBN-13 (pbk): 978-1-4842-1924-9   ISBN-13 (electronic): 978-1-4842-1925-6
DOI 10.1007/978-1-4842-1925-6

Library of Congress Control Number: 2016961817

Managing Director: Welmoed Spahr
Lead Editor: Todd Green
Technical Reviewer: Abhishek Gupta
Editorial Board: Steve Anglin, Pramila Balan, Laura Berendson, Aaron Black, Louise Corrigan, Jonathan Gennick, Todd Green, Robert Hutchinson, Celestin Suresh John, Nikhil Karkal, James Markham, Susan McDermott, Matthew Moodie, Natalie Pao, Gwenan Spearing
Coordinating Editor: Jill Balzano
Copy Editor: Corbin Collins
Compositor: SPi Global
Indexer: SPi Global
Artist: SPi Global

Distributed to the book trade worldwide by Springer Science+Business Media New York, 233 Spring Street, 6th Floor, New York, NY 10013. Phone 1-800-SPRINGER, fax (201) 348-4505, e-mail orders-ny@springer-sbm.com, or visit www.springer.com. Apress Media, LLC is a California LLC and the sole member (owner) is Springer Science + Business Media Finance Inc (SSBM Finance Inc). SSBM Finance Inc is a **Delaware** corporation.

For information on translations, please e-mail rights@apress.com, or visit www.apress.com.

Apress and friends of ED books may be purchased in bulk for academic, corporate, or promotional use. eBook versions and licenses are also available for most titles. For more information, reference our Special Bulk Sales–eBook Licensing web page at www.apress.com/bulk-sales.

Any source code or other supplementary materials referenced by the author in this text are available to readers at www.apress.com. For detailed information about how to locate your book's source code, go to www.apress.com/source-code/. Readers can also access source code at SpringerLink in the Supplementary Material section for each chapter.

Printed on acid-free paper

To Mou, for never giving up on me

Contents at a Glance

Contents

Foreword

The world of programming used to be simple.

We had merely our own stuff to care for. We could proudly claim we knew everything there was to know about the code we wrote and maintained. At worst, all we had to do was to go and peek. It was all in the source code, in small enough volumes for us to massage it, understand it, master it entirely. We knew what to look for. We knew where to look.

It was a much simpler world indeed.

Because things have changed dramatically. We routinely manage code we inherit, code we download, code other people write. Even the code we write ourselves is growing much faster than it did before. We are way past the stage where our knowledge is a reliable-enough oracle for the facts buried in our code. We are also long past the stage where we can perform changes across the board, just by being super good with a text editor, macros, shortcuts, and all. Because of volume, because of complexity, large-scale refactorings have turned to software projects in their own right.

For a long time, metaprogramming (writing programs that operate on other programs) has been a nerdish way for software engineers to keep busy, but it has now come to industrial relevance. One cannot rely on human knowledge and work power to gather accurate information about software systems, and even less transform them systematically. They have just gotten too big, too complex, and are evolving too fast for the roll-your-sleeves-up-and-get-going attitude to be an option any longer. One must be able to automate many tasks that analyze and/or transform non-trivial software systems.

To compound the difficulty, until recently, metaprogramming required highly specialized tools and equally specialized languages. That should not come as a surprise: Would you really want to write COBOL code to process a COBOL program in any non-trivial way? Or even C for C programs? This gap of abstraction and sophistication between the languages one processes and the languages one uses to develop such metaprograms has seriously limited the adoption of metaprogramming in the industry. It was a niche thing.

This book, together with Roslyn, are major contributions to get metaprogramming out of this niche status. They don't just advocate and demonstrate metaprogramming as a generic technique, but focus on circular meta-programming, where a widely used general-purpose language is used to manipulate real-world programs written in this same language.

It is not the first such circular effort though: The now defunct Jackpot project aimed to do exactly that for Java, and I can only think of the market's maturity as an explanation for Roslyn's momentum and success in comparison. Even before Jackpot, circular metaprogramming was not unheard of, but was limited to more marginal languages such as Prolog, Lisp, Smalltalk, or YAFL (developed by yours truly).

Sudipta's demonstration is only marginally about what he achieves using C#, Roslyn, and LINQ, building on his previous book on the topic. Anyone (including myself) could argue about the merits of the problems he solves, his approach, and his solutions, but that would be missing the whole point. His book is all about demonstrating how Roslyn and LINQ have made metaprogramming simple. It does not have to be a highly specialized activity any longer. It can and should be part of every serious software developer's toolbox.

Nowhere is this point about DIY metaprogramming more obvious than in the chapter about visualization, where he shows how one can connect with existing (often freely available) software components to best depict whatever it is he wants to emphasize, demonstrate, isolate—in a nutshell, visualize. In a few dozen lines of code, he shows how the most intricate, project-specific metric or factoid can be rendered effectively.

In this area, I am personally into arrow and graphs more than dots of varying magnitude, pie, and bar charts. All a matter of taste. Quite logically, graphviz is my logical favorite rendition tool.

But my opinion is irrelevant. And with all due respect, so is Sudipta's. What really matters is your opinion, and how you can put metaprogramming to the best use possible to solve the problems you face, address your concerns, integrate in your environment, and adapt to your ways of working and thinking. And on your way to get there, this book is an invaluable contribution.

—Dr. Darius Blasband, CEO raincode.com

About the Author

Sudipta Mukherjee is an experienced programmer, born in Shibpur, a town in the Howrah district of West Bengal in India. He grew up in Bally, another small town in the Howrah district. He has been working with Roslyn since the first CTP release and is an enthusiastic advocate for building source code analysis systems. Sudipta is a prolific author. His previous books include *Data Structures Using C* (http://goo.gl/pttSh), *.NET 4.0 Generics: Beginner's Guide* (http://goo.gl/LwVmZ5), *F# for Machine Learning Essentials* (http://amzn.to/2bAUG5i), and *Thinking in LINQ* (http://amzn.to/2e2YEUq). His interests include data structures, algorithms, text processing, machine learning, natural language processing, programming languages, and tools development. When not working at his day job or writing books, Sudipta likes to spend time with his family and follow his passions of sketching and painting. Sudipta lives in Bangalore and can be contacted via email at sudipto80@yahoo.com or on Twitter, at @samthecoder.

About the Technical Reviewer

Abhishek Gupta is an Azure and Xamarin Specialist with seven years of corporate work experience, including three years at Microsoft Hyderabad. His knowledge areas include algorithms and data structures, operating systems, basics of machine learning, cloud computing, and smartphone app development for Android, iOS, and Windows Phone. He is interested mainly in Microsoft technologies. Abhishek loves learning new technologies and frameworks, and most of the time finds himself getting his hands dirty in new APIs. Whenever he has free time, he loves driving to places full of nature, trekking, and writing blogs (which you can read at `http://cloudandmobile.in`).

Acknowledgments

First, I want to thank the Microsoft Roslyn team for constantly evolving the API to make it cover more features of C#. As this book is being written, the next version of the C# compiler is being built using Roslyn. If you have ever tried to create analyzers for source code and been faced with the enormous challenge of writing your own parsers, then this book is for you, and Roslyn is your savior.

Although my name appears on the book as author, this book wouldn't have been possible without the support from my editors at Apress. I especially want to mention Jill Balzano and Todd Green for being patient and supportive when I missed some of the deadlines for chapter delivery. Thank you both for being nice and kind.

I want to thank Dr. Darius Blasband, CEO of Raincode (`www.raincode.com`) for kindly writing the foreword.

Last but not the least, I want to thank my wife Mou for always being there and being supportive. Since last time, my son graduated. He's now potty trained. So much has changed since this picture was taken. He is taller, sharper.

What hasn't changed, though, is his love for computers and typing. Here is what he typed, sitting on my computer.

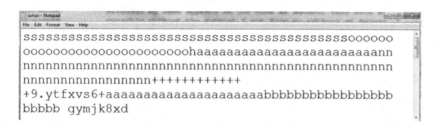

I saved the file by his name. He now learned to type his name but is not quite accustomed to the feather touch keyboard yet—that's why all the duplicate characters. I think when I write again, he will start programming.

Finally, I want to thank my Lord for giving me courage and dreams!

Introduction

Metaprogramming is programming to analyze another program. The biggest challenge in doing metaprogramming is being able to understand the program. To understand the program, we must be able to parse the program. But parsing is a non-trivial process, and good quality parsers have been living inside the compiler ever since.

So, compilers used to see it all. They saw the source code and generated the parse tree and finally the machine instructions. However, everything happened inside the compiler and therefore couldn't be re-used. Worse, compilers used to forget everything after generating the machine-executible instructions.

Meet Roslyn from Microsoft. It changes all that. Roslyn is a compiler-as-a-service. That means we can now tap into the enormous knowledge generated by the compiler, ask intelligent and deep questions about the code, and build analyzers for given source code more easily than ever before. Roslyn removed the barriers for metaprogramming.

This book will not teach you all of Roslyn—Roslyn is huge. But it will teach you some part of the Syntax Parsing API and how to use it to generate several code-related metrics. You will see how these generated results can be glued to beautiful state-of-the-art data visualization using the JavaScript framework to be rendered on your browser. By the way, as I write this Roslyn is in active development, so if you see that some query is not running, please drop me a line and I'll help you. All the source code is available for download from Apress.

Sound exciting? Please start reading. I bet you will enjoy it!

CHAPTER 1

▪ ▪ ▪

Meet Roslyn Syntax API

Until recently the biggest challenge for metaprogramming in .NET was that there was not a decent C# parser that could have been used to parse C# programs with confidence and keep up with the modifications made in the language specification. Some companies and individuals (including yours truly) have had to write their own parser to parse C# source code—because parsing is the first step to analyzing source code. Till Roslyn came into picture, compilers used to be like black boxes. Source code used to go at one end, and machine instructions/executibles came out the other end. However, in parsing code, compilers gained lot of knowledge, all of which used to get lost in the process. This knowledge could have served as the basis for writing analyzers.

In this chapter I walk you through some of the key types in the Roslyn Syntax Parsing API for C#. Knowledge of these types will be essential to be able to follow along with examples in the rest of the book.

One important thing you may note when working with Roslyn is that Roslyn has special names for coding constructs—different than what you know from your coding experience. For example, any *node* apart from code node is called *trivia*, and a *comment* is a type of a trivia. If you take a primer class in compiler design, it will start to make sense why some of the types are named the way they are; however, for general purpose of writing the analyzers it is not needed.

After reading this chapter you should be able to make sense of several types in Roslyn Syntax Parsing API, be able to appreciate their existence, and potentially be in a position to apply this knowledge to write your own analyzers for source code—and follow along examples for the rest of the book.

The following sections walk you through some of the important methods of the SyntaxTree class that are used more frequently than others while writing the analyzers.

Syntax Tree Methods

I have used LINQPad to capture the tool-tips so you see the general usages and the signature of the methods.

GetRoot

This method gets the root of the syntax tree. This is the first step to write any analyzer. See how this method is used in Figure 1-1.

Electronic supplementary material The online version of this chapter (doi:10.1007/978-1-4842-1925-6_1) contains supplementary material, which is available to authorized users.

S. Mukherjee, *Source Code Analytics With Roslyn and JavaScript Data Visualization*, DOI 10.1007/978-1-4842-1925-6_1

```
var tree = CSharpSyntaxTree.ParseText(code);

tree.GetRoot(
```

Microsoft.CodeAnalysis.SyntaxNode SyntaxTree.GetRoot ([CancellationToken **cancellationToken** = default(CancellationToken)])
Gets the root node of the syntax tree, causing computation if necessary.
F1 for help

Figure 1-1. *Showing how GetRoot() is called along with signature*

DescendantNodes

This method fetches all the child nodes of the root nodes. These nodes are all syntax nodes and not the trivia nodes. Figure 1-2 shows how this method is used.

```
var tree = CSharpSyntaxTree.ParseText(code);

tree.GetRoot()
    .DescendantNodes(
```

▲ 2 of 2 ▾ IEnumerable<Microsoft.CodeAnalysis.SyntaxNode> SyntaxNode.DescendantNodes (
TextSpan **span,**
[Func<Microsoft.CodeAnalysis.SyntaxNode, bool> **descendIntoChildren** = null],
[bool descendIntoTrivia = False])
Gets a list of descendant nodes in prefix document order.
span: The span the node's full span must intersect. **F1 for help**

Figure 1-2. *Showing how DescendantNodes() is called along with signature*

DescendantTrivia

This method fetches all the trivia nodes of the current node on which this method is called. These nodes are all trivia nodes. Trivia is ignored by the compiler but can be really useful for analyzing source code. Figure 1-3 shows how this method can be used.

```
var tree = CSharpSyntaxTree.ParseText(code);

tree.GetRoot()
    .DescendantTrivia(
```

▲ 1 of 2 ▾ IEnumerable<Microsoft.CodeAnalysis.SyntaxTrivia> SyntaxNode.DescendantTrivia (
[Func<**Microsoft.CodeAnalysis.SyntaxNode, bool> descendIntoChildren** = null],
[bool descendIntoTrivia = False])
Get a list of all the trivia associated with the descendant nodes and tokens.
F1 for help

Figure 1-3. *Showing usage of DescendantTrivia() method*

DescendantTokens

This method gets all the descendant tokens of the current node. These tokens also include the trivia nodes. Figure 1-4) shows how this method can be used.

```
var tree = CSharpSyntaxTree.ParseText(code);

tree.GetRoot()
    .DescendantTokens(
```

```
▲ 1 of 2 ▼  IEnumerable<Microsoft.CodeAnalysis.SyntaxToken> SyntaxNode.DescendantTokens (
            [Func<Microsoft.CodeAnalysis.SyntaxNode, bool> descendIntoChildren = null],
            [bool descendIntoTrivia = False])
Gets a list of all the tokens in the span of this node.
F1 for help
```

Figure 1-4. *Showing usage of the DescendantTokens() method*

Ancestors

This method gets all the ancestors of the current node. This method is useful to go back to find the parent node of a given kind of a node in question. For example, Figure 1-5 shows how this method can be used to find all the ancestors of the first method declaration found in the given source code in the variable code.

```
var tree = CSharpSyntaxTree.ParseText(code);

tree.GetRoot()
    .DescendantNodes()
    .OfType<MethodDeclarationSyntax>()
    .First()
    .Ancestors(
```

```
IEnumerable<Microsoft.CodeAnalysis.SyntaxNode> SyntaxNode.Ancestors (
        [bool ascendOutOfTrivia = True])
Gets a list of ancestor nodes
F1 for help
```

Figure 1-5. *Showing usage of Ancestors() method to locate parents of interest*

Important Types

Now that you are well equipped with several useful SyntaxTree methods it is about time that you learn about some of the important *types* in the framework. Knowledge about these types will be crucial to following along the example for the rest of the book. This list is by no means comprehensive, but it will get you started so that you can write your analyzers and follow along with the examples in the rest of the book.

MethodDeclarationSyntax

This type represents the method of a class/type.

- Arity: The number of generic types on which the method is described.
- AttributeLists: List of attributes applied on the method.
- Body: Body.Statements gives all the statements described in the method.
- ConstraintClauses: Constraints on the generic types of the method.

- `ExplicitInterfaceSpecifier`: Check to see if this method is an explicit interface specifier or not.

- `Identifier`: Name of the method is stored in this variable.

- `Modifiers`: Represents list of modifiers (public/private/protected/static) of the method.

- `ParameterList`: This property represents the list of parameters that are taken by the method.

- `TypeParameterList`: If the `Arity` of a method is more than zero, then this list will have all the details about those parameters.

Figure 1-6 puts these attributes of `MethodDeclarationSyntax` in perspective. Reconciling this figure with the definitions of these fields just given, you see how these are mapped. As mentioned earlier, naming in Roslyn may sound little bit off if you don't have a formal introduction to compiler design. It may be difficult to mentally map the name `Identifier` to the name of the method. However, that's how it is designed. The name of everything is wrapped into the attribute of a class called `Identifier`. The name of a class will be thus available inside the `Identifier` of `ClassDeclarationSyntax` type instance.

```
[Obsolete("Don't use anymore")]/*AttributeLists*/
public static /*Modifiers*/
       int /*Return Type*/
       GetID /*Identifier*/
       <T>/*Arity*/
       /*ParameterList*/
       (T customerName, string location)
        where T:class /*Constraint Clauses*/
{
    /*Body*/
    // Do stuff
    return 0;
}
```

Figure 1-6. *Annotated method body with different parts*

ClassDeclarationSyntax

This type represents the class declarations in source code.

- `Arity`: Arity is the number of generic types on which the class is described.

- `AttributeLists`: List of attributes applied on the class.

- `BaseList`: This property represents the list of base classes and interfaces that this type inherits from or implements.

- `ConstraintClauses`: This property represents the constraint clauses to be attributed on this type.

- `Identifier`: This property holds the name of this type. This is universal across Roslyn. The identifier property of any type holds the name (if applicable) for that particular type.

- Members: This property represents all the members of the class.

- Modifiers: Represents list of modifiers (public/private/protected/static) of the class.

Figure 1-7 puts all these properties in perspective.

```
public /* Modifiers */
class Something /* Identifier */
      <T> /* Typed Parameter or Arity */
      :ICloneable /* BaseList */
   where T : IDisposable /* */
{
    /*Members*/
    void doSomethingPrivately()
    {

    }
    object ICloneable.Clone()
    {
        return this;
    }
}
```

Figure 1-7. *Annotated class with different parts*

SructDeclarationSyntax

This type represents a structure declaration node in the given source code. This type has similar properties like that of ClassDeclarationSyntax, but their meaning remains same in the context for a struct. So in Figure 1-7, if you replace the class with a struct, all the other parts make sense for structure declaration.

InterfaceDeclarationSyntax

This type represents an interface declaration node in the given source code. This type has similar properties like that of ClassDeclarationSyntax, but their meaning remains same in the context for a struct. So in Figure 1-7, if you replace the class with an interface, all the other parts make sense for interface declaration.

IndexerDeclarationSyntax

This type represents an indexer defined in a type.

- AccessorList: This property represents all the accessors of the indexer.

- AttributeLists: This property represents all the attributes of the indexer.

- ExplicitInterfaceSpecifier: This property returns true if the indexer is marked explicitly as an interface specfier.

- Modifiers: Represents list of modifiers (public/private/protected/static) of the indexer.

- ParameterList: Represents list of parameters taken by the indexer.

- Type: Represents the return type of the indexer.

Figure 1-8 shows these properties for a sample indexer definition.

```
public /* Modifiers */
T   /* Type */
this[int i /* ParameterList */]
{
    /* Accessors */
    get
    {
        return arr[i];
    }
    set
    {
        arr[i] = value;
    }
}
```

Figure 1-8. *Showing parts of an annotated indexer*

PropertyDeclarationSyntax

This type represents property declarations in class/type definitions. This is very similar to IndexerDeclarationSyntax, but it doesn't have the ParameterList because properties don't accept any parameter—meaning for all other properties of this type, is similar to that of IndexerDeclarationSyntax. Figure 1-9 shows parts of annotated property declaration syntax.

```
public /* Modifiers */
int  /* Type */
Month /* Identifier */
{
    /* AccesorList */
    get
    {
        return month;
    }
    set
    {
        if ((value > 0) && (value < 13))
        {
            month = value;
        }
    }
}
```

Figure 1-9. *Showing parts of an annotated propery declaration*

ForStatementSyntax

This type represents the for loop syntax.

- Condition: Represents the condition to terminate the loop.

- Declaration: This represents the variable declarations inside the loop. Sometimes looping variables are declared inside the loop and initialized.

- Incrementors: This represents the part of the loop that increments or decremenets the value of the looping variables.

- Initializers: This represents the part of the loop that initializes the looping variables.

- Statement: This represents the actual body of the loop.

Figure 1-10 shows part of an annotated for loop.

```
for (int i = 1, j = -1 /* Declaration */ ;
        i <= 50 /* Condition */ ;
        i++,j-- /* Incrementors */)
{
    Console.WriteLine(i); /* Statement */
}
```

Figure 1-10. *Showing parts of an annotated for loop*

When the declarations are done before the loop begins, then the value for Declaration becomes null and all values are made avaialble inside Initializers, as shown in Figure 1-11.

```
int i = 0,  j = 0;
for (i = 1, j = -1 /* Initializers */ ;
        i <= 50 /* Condition */ ;
        i++,j-- /* Incrementors */)
{
    Console.WriteLine(i); /* Statement */
}
```

Figure 1-11. *Showing parts of an annotated for loop where loop variables are declared outside of the loop*

ConstructorDeclarationSyntax

This represents constructors of a class.

- AttributeLists: List of attributes on this particular instance of constructor.

- Body: This represents the actual body of the constructor.

- Modifiers: This represents the modifiers (public, private, and so on) of the constructor.

- ParameterList: List of parameters taken by this specific constructor.

7

Figure 1-12 shows parts of an annotated constructor definition.

```
public /* Modifiers */
Employee /* Identifier */
(int weeklySalary, int numberOfWeeks /* ParameterList */)
    : this(weeklySalary * numberOfWeeks)
{
}
```

Figure 1-12. *Showing parts of an annotated constructor*

ForEachStatementSyntax

This type represents the foreach statements.

- Expression: This represents the expression over which the enumeration has to be performed by the foreach loop.

- Identifier: This holds the name of the looping varible.

- Statement: This represents the actual body of the loop.

- Type: This holds the type of the looping variable.

Figure 1-13 shows the annotated foreach statement syntax.

```
foreach (string z /* Identifier */
          in
          names /* Expression */ )
    Console.WriteLine(z); /* Statement */
```

Figure 1-13. *Showing parts of foreach loop*

SwitchStatementSyntax

This type represents switch statements or switch blocks.

- Expression: This represents the expression on which the switching has to happen.

- Sections: This property represents actual sections of a switch block

Figure 1-14 shows parts of a switch block.

```
int caseSwitch = 1;
switch (caseSwitch /* Expression */ )
{
    /* Sections */
    case 1:
        Console.WriteLine("Case 1");
        break;
    case 2:
        Console.WriteLine("Case 2");
        break;
    default:
        Console.WriteLine("Default case");
        break;
}
```

Figure 1-14. *Showing parts of a* switch *statement*

ParameterSyntax

In some of the previous types you have seen a property called ParameterList. This is nothing but a list of all parameters expressed as ParameterSyntax. If we want to find details about any individual parameter, we need to use this type.

- Default: This represents whether the parameter is default or not.

- Identifier: This holds the given name of the parameter.

- Type: The type of the parameter.

Figure 1-15 shows an annotated parameter list for a method.

```
public decimal CalculateTax
(
    decimal income, /* Identifier : income, Type : decimal */
    decimal insurance,
    bool married,
    bool hasKids = false /* Identifier : hasKids, Type : bool , Default : true*/ )
{
    return decimal.MaxValue;
}
```

Figure 1-15. *Showing parameter details for a method*

DoStatementSyntax

This type represents the do loop syntax.

- Condition: This represents the condition of the loop based on which it has to terminate.

- Statement: This represents the statement of the loop—in other words, the body of the loop.

Figure 1-16 shows an annotated do loop.

```
double diff = 10;
do
{
    /*Statement*/|
    diff--;
    Console.WriteLine(diff);
}while(diff!=0 /* Condition */);
```

Figure 1-16. *Showing annotated do loop*

UsingStatementSyntax

This type represents the using blocks. If a type that implements IDisposable interface is wrapped inside a using block, then the garbage collection happens automatically on exit of the using block. This is a very common pattern in .NET code.

- Declaration: This represents the variable declaration inside the using block where the type that implements the IDisposable interface is instantiated.

- Expression: This represents the expression of creating the IDisposable instance inside the using block. The variable can be created either by a straight constructor or by a factory method or such. If it is created by a straight constructor, then this property is left null.

- Statement: This represents the actual code inside the using block.

Figure 1-17 shows annotated using block.

```
void Main()
{
    using (SystemResource resource = new SystemResource() /* Declaration */)
    {
        Console.WriteLine(1); /* Statement */|
    }
}
class SystemResource : IDisposable
{
    public void Dispose()
    {
        // The implementation of this method not described here.
        // ... For now, just report the call.
        Console.WriteLine(0);
    }
}
```

Figure 1-17. *Showing annotated using statement block*

IfStatementSyntax

This type represents the if statement syntax.

- Condition: This holds the condition of the if statement.

- Else: This represents an alternate path should the condition evaluate to false.

- Statement: This represents the actual code inside the if block.

Figure 1-18 shows an annoated if block.

```
if (price < 10 /* Condition */)
    /* Statement */
    Console.WriteLine("Price is low");
else /* Else */
    Console.WriteLine("Price is high");
```

Figure 1-18. *Showing annotated if statement*

TryStatementSyntax

This type represents the try-catch-finally blocks.

- Block: This represents the code that is wrapped inside the try block

- Catches: This represents the list of catch blocks.

- Finally: This represents the finally block.

Figure 1-19 shows the try-catch-finally block.

```
void ReadFile(int index)
{
    // To run this code, substitute a valid path from your local machine
    string path = @"c:\users\public\test.txt";
    System.IO.StreamReader file = new System.IO.StreamReader(path);
    char[] buffer = new char[10];
    try
    {
        /* Block */
        file.ReadBlock(buffer, index, buffer.Length);
    }
    /* Catches */
    catch (System.IO.IOException e)
    {

        Console.WriteLine("Error reading from {0}. Message = {1}", path, e.Message);
    }
    catch (Exception ex)
    {

    }
    /* Finally */          |
    finally
    {
        if (file != null)
        {
            file.Close();
        }
    }
    // Do something with buffer...
}
```

Figure 1-19. *Showing annotated* `try-catch-finally` *block*

LocalDeclarationStatementSyntax

This represents the local variable declarations inside a method/class.

- `Declaration`: This represents the variable declaration.

- `IsConst`: Returns `true` if the variable being declared is constant, `false` otherwise.

Figure 1-20 shows annotated local variable declaration.

```
public void funny(int x)
{
    //identifier: z, type :int , value : 0
    int z = 0;
    //identifier : t, type : int, IsConst : false
    int y = x + 1;
    //identifier: w, type : double, IsConst: true
    const double w = 2.13423545;

    //Do Something
}
```

Figure 1-20. *Showing some local variable declaration*

ConditionalExpressionSyntax

This type represents a conditional expression.

- Condition: This represents the condition on which the ternary operation has to be performed.

- WhenFalse: This represents the action to be executed when the condition is not satisfied/false.

- WhenTrue: This represents the action to be executed when the condition is satisfied/true.

Figure 1-21 shows an annotated ternary expression.

```
void fun()
{
    int x = 0;

    int z = x > 3 /* Condition */
            ? x - 3 /* WhenTrue */
            : 1 /* WhenFalse */ ;
}
```

Figure 1-21. *Showing annotated conditional expression*

ParenthesizedLambdaExpressionSyntax

This type represents lambda expressions with parenthesis.

- Body: This represents the body of the lambda expression.

- ParameterList: This holds the details about the parameters passed to the lambda expression.

Figure 1-22 shows the details of parenthesized lambda expression syntax.

```
class A
{
    Func<int, int, bool> ch = (a, b) /* ParameterList */
                => a == b /* Body */;
}
```

Figure 1-22. *Showing annotated parenthesized lambda expression syntax*

WhileStatementSyntax

This type represents the while looping construct.

- Condition: This represents the condition of the loop.

- Statement: This holds statements to be executed as long as the loop runs.

Figure 1-23 shows an annotated while statement.

```
while (price > 10 /* Condition */)
{
    price--; /* Statement */
}
```

Figure 1-23. *Showing annotated while loop*

Summary

In this chapter you got acquantainted with the basics of Roslyn Syntax API for parsing C# source code. Although a portion of the Roslyn Syntax API classes and methods are declared, you should now have a general idea of how this API is structured.

It is beyond the scope of the book to list all the types of the syntax API and list their purposes, but be assured that there exists a class to deal with every feature of C# and VB.NET.

In the rest of the book, you will see how these API types and methods are used to create useful analyzers to extract insight from the given source code.

Code forensics is an active area of research, and as you have seen, it uses lot of machine learning. kNN is used in the chapter, but the accuracy is much better if a neural network is fed the data. Currently, Deep Learning is becoming commonplace. So, using those technologies also can yield a better result. Elements of style should reflect the habits of the developer/programmer—something that they can't change without trying real hard. A programmer who is inclined to choose Pascal case names will not choose camel case names, even when trying hard to avoid getting caught for plagarization.

CHAPTER 2

■ ■ ■

Code Quality Metrics

Source code is the biggest asset of software companies. However, that asset can get rusty over time. In software design, these rusts are known as *code smells*. This chapter will show you how to find such code smells from your source code using Roslyn and LINQ.

Artists sometimes pause after they've been painting a while and step back. They relax and look at their painting. This gives them a clue whether they are doing what it takes to get to the picture of what they had been envisioning. We programmers can take a cue from our painter friends. While developing programs, developers can pause for a while to see whether we are getting where we wanted to go. However, till now all the resources we had worked on compiled assemblies. That means we couldn't have checked the state as we go (from uncompilable source). Thanks to Microsoft, Roslyn changed that. With the Roslyn Syntax API, we can check our code as we build it—much like our artist friends.

For example, having dead code as part of the comments is an example of *code clutter*. On the other hand, having multiple nested loops or branching statements (sometimes call a *bow and arrow* pattern) are examples of *bad software design*, and a namespace with 40 classes has a high *conceptual load*, meaning it takes a lot to comprehend what that namespace is trying to do. Same is true for a class with huge list of methods.

Each of the code smells discussed in this chapter starts with the name of the smell in the heading followed by a little description of the smell. For explaining each code smell, I use toy example code. I used the word *toy* because most of these codes are fabricated by yours truly and may not make sense by themselves. However, they play an important role in explaining the concept of the smell. In a nutshell, the code examples you see in these toy examples may look stupid, may not make sense, or may be incomplete—but they are helpful to hammer home the point I want to make.

Next I show how you can use the Roslyn Syntax API and LINQ to check whether the toy example code has the mentioned code smell or not. The takeaway is that you can use that same code to run on your own code. So, the examples are ready to be used as is.

At last I present the output of the script that I wrote using Roslyn and LINQ, followed by an explanation of how the script works. I hope this explanation will give you enough ideas to use Roslyn and LINQ on your own settings. In order to explain the code we need to walk through the code, and in order to make that code walkthrough simple, I have marked significant milestones in the code with annotations like //#1, //#2, and so on in comments. I'll follow it throughout the book as I did in Chapter 1.

Finally, each code smell is categorized in any of the four categories already mentioned. By the way, there is no arrangement. The order in which these code smells are described is ad hoc.

I have annotated the first code smell with all these parts so that you know where to expect which one.

Most of the code smells apply to classes, namespaces, and more, but for the demonstration purpose, I have chosen to find these metrics on one of these, and you can always extend that.

© Sudipta Mukherjee 2016
S. Mukherjee, *Source Code Analytics With Roslyn and JavaScript Data Visualization*,
DOI 10.1007/978-1-4842-1925-6_2

Setting Up LINQPad to Use Roslyn

LINQPad will be used to execute the scripts in this chapter. This section will guide you to configure LINQPad so that you can run these queries smoothly.

1. Download LINQPad if you don't have it already

2. Create a C# console project in Visual Studio and download the following NuGet package using the Package Manager console from Tools ➤ Package Manager Console.

   ```
   Install-Package Microsoft.CodeAnalysis.CSharp
   ```

3. Find the locations of these libraries by right-clicking the properties on the added NuGet reference in the C# project.

   ```
   Microsoft.CodeAnalysis
   Microsoft.CodeAnalysis.CSharp
   Microsoft.CodeAnalysis.CSharp.Syntax
   ```

4. Open LINQPad and press F4 to add these references, as shown in Figure 2-1.

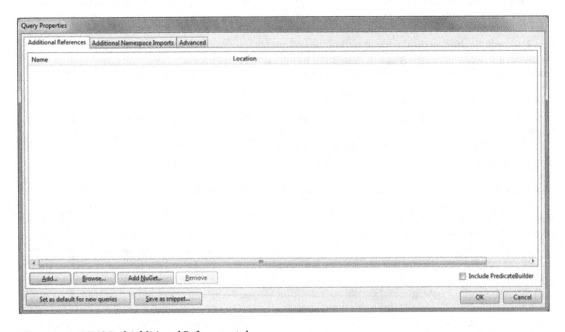

Figure 2-1. *LINQPad Additional References tab*

5. Locate the assembly and add, as shown in Figure 2-2.

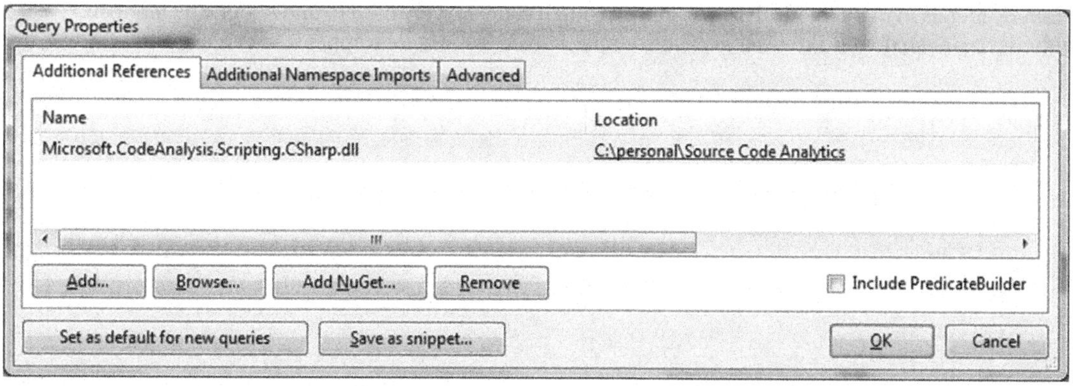

Figure 2-2. *Adding a reference to Roslyn*

6. Click the Additional Namespace Imports tab and add the namespace shown in Figure 2-3 there.

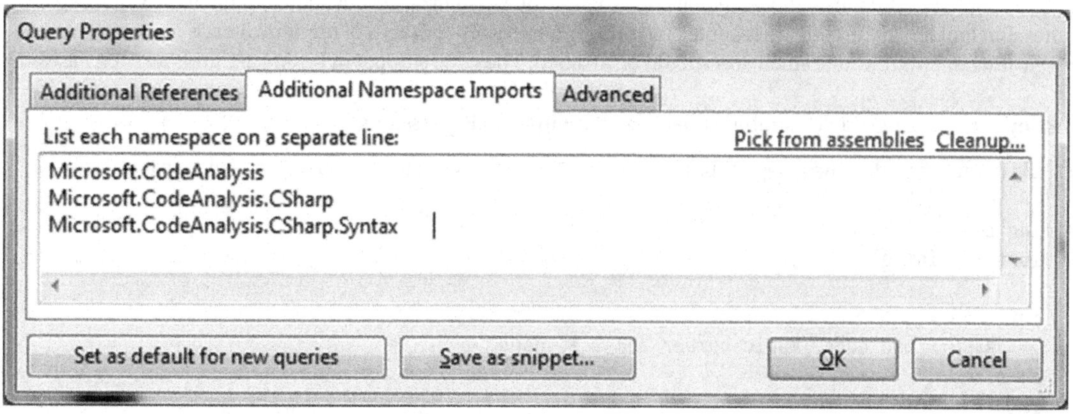

Figure 2-3. *Adding namespaces in LINQPad*

7. Click the "Set as default for new queries" button and then click OK.

That's it for setting up LINQPad for running all the queries in the book.

If you have a licensed copy of LINQPad, you don't have to do these steps and can directly download and integrate the NuGet package by clicking the Add NuGet button and locating Microsoft.CodeAnalysis.CSharp.dll from NuGet.

Magic Numbers in Mathematics

Numeric literals in mathematical expressions in source code are very hard to understand, let alone fix, without very deep domain knowledge. For example, consider the code snippet shown in Figure 2-4.

```
float fun(int g)
{
    int size = 10000;
    g+=23456;
    g+=size;
    return g/10;
}
```

Figure 2-4. *Magic number usages in source code*

From Figure 2-4 can you tell what the meaning of 23456 is? You may not know why size is added to g but you know for a fact that size is being added to g when you see the code g+=size. The point is, without metadata it is impossible to figure out the meaning of a given numeric value. Same is true for the call g/10. Here 10 could be someone's shoe size or it could be the the normalization constant to reduce the value of g ten times. But looking at the code we can't tell anything. These types of usages of numeric literals are known as *magic usages*. This is a code smell and should be avoided. The code snippet in Listing 2-1 finds all such cases.

Listing 2-1. Finding Magic Number Usages in Mathematical Expressions

```
//Following script finds magic lines for +=, -=, *=, /= and + , //- , * and / cases

string code =
@"float fun(int g)
{
    int size = 10000;
    g+=23456;//bad code. magic number 23456 is used.
    g+=size;
    return g/10;
}
decimal updateRate(decimal rate)
{
    return rate / 0.2345M;
}
decimal updateRateM(decimal rateM)
{
  decimal basis = 0.2345M;
        return rateM/basis;
}";
List<SyntaxKind> kinds = new List<SyntaxKind>()
{
 SyntaxKind.AddAssignExpression,//+=
 SyntaxKind.SubtractAssignExpression,//-=
```

```
SyntaxKind.MultiplyAssignExpression,//*=
SyntaxKind.DivideAssignExpression, // /=
SyntaxKind.AddExpression, // +
SyntaxKind.SubtractExpression,// -
SyntaxKind.MultiplyExpression,// *
SyntaxKind.DivideExpression // /
};
CSharpSyntaxTree.ParseText(code)
      .GetRoot()
      .DescendantNodes()
       .Where (st => st.Kind == SyntaxKind.MethodDeclaration)
       .Cast<MethodDeclarationSyntax>()
       .Select (st =>
          new
          {
               MethodName = st.Identifier.ValueText,//#1
               MagicLines =
            CSharpSyntaxTree.ParseText(st.ToFullString())
                     .GetRoot()
                     .DescendantNodes()
                     .Where (z => kinds
                            .Any (k => k == z.Kind()))
                     .Select (q => q.ToFullString().Trim())
                  .Where(w => CSharpSyntaxTree
                    .ParseText("void dummy(){"+w.ToString()+"}")
                    .GetRoot()
                    .DescendantTokens()
                    .Any(s => //#2
                       s.Kind == SyntaxKind.NumericLiteralToken))
}).Dump("Magic lines. Please avoid these");
```

That listing's code produces the output shown in Figure 2-5.

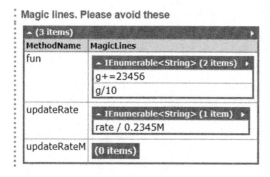

Figure 2-5. *Mathematical expressions that use magic numbers*

The line marked #1 finds the method name, and the line marked #2 checks whether the method uses any magic number represented by NumericLiteralToken.

Magic Numbers Used in Index

Sometimes we want to access a particular element from a given index in a dictionary or a map. Let's say as per the current logic the data is always exptected to be available at the fourth index of an array. If you find that the code is trying to get the element from the array by arrayName[3] then you should change that because that's a code smell. There is no gurantee that the item will be available there at the fourth index always.

Listing 2-2 finds methods that fail this test.

Listing 2-2. Finding Magic Number Usages in Indices

```
string code =
@"int fun(int b)
  {
      int x = 323;
      int z = dic[x] + x + dic[323];
      return z + b;
  }
  float funny(float c)
  {
      int d = 234;
      Dictionary<float,string> dic = getDic();
      float z = dic[d];
      return z;
  }

  Dictionary<float,string> getDic()
  {
          return new Dictionary<float,string>();
  }
";

var tree = CSharpSyntaxTree.ParseText(code);

tree.GetRoot()
.DescendantNodes()
.OfType<BracketedArgumentListSyntax>()
.Select(bals =>
   new
     {
        Method = bals.Ancestors()
             .OfType<MethodDeclarationSyntax>()
             .First()
             .Identifier.ValueText,
        Indices = bals.Arguments
                 .Select(a => a.GetText()
                   .Container
                   .CurrentText
                   .ToString())
   })
```

```
//Find defaulter methods that use magic indices
.Where(bals =>
    bals.Indices
        .Any(i => Regex.Match(i,"[0-9]+").Success))
.Dump ("Methods using magic indices");
```

That code produces the output as shown in Figure 2-6.

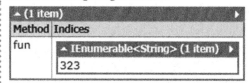

Figure 2-6. *Method that uses magic indices*

Thus the script identifies rightly that the function fun uses magic number as index.

Magic Numbers Used in Conditions

Sometimes magic numbers are used in conditional statements. Although trivial usages are okay, un-intuitive usage of magic numbers in conditional statements makes those very difficult (if at all possible) to fully comprehend.

Take a look at the function definitions shown in Figure 2-7.

```
bool hasElements(List<string> elements)
{
    return elements.Count > 0;
}

bool hasSuchElements(List<Elements> elements)
{
    return elements.Any( z => z.Stock > 45);
}
```

Figure 2-7. *Examples of magic numbers used in conditions*

The first function is trivial, and it's okay to use 0 to check that the collection is not empty. However, the usage of magic number 45 in the second function can lead to confusion. Although some developers may argue that it is pretty clear from the statement that it has been looking for elements where the value of Stock is greater than 45, that's not sufficient. What's the meaning or context of using 45? What does 45 signify? It's impossible to figure out from the code what 45 means. Instead consider the code shown in Figure 2-8.

```
int LOWEST_STOCK_LIMIT = 45;

bool hasSuchElements(List<Elements> elements)
{
    return elements.Any( z => z.Stock > LOWEST_STOCK_LIMIT);
}
```

Figure 2-8. *Replacing magic numbers by constants*

The following code listing finds such usages of magic numbers in conditions.

Listing 2-3. Finding Magic Number Usages in Conditions

```
//Magic numbers in numeric condition is bad
//because they are hard to understand and thus replace
string code =
@"class PasswordManager
  {
      int x = 8;
      bool IsGood(string password)
      {
          if(password.Length < 5)
                return false;
            return password.Length >= 7;
      }
      int fun()
      {
          return g[x];
      }
      bool zun()
      {
          if(z > 3.4)
            return false;
          else
            return true;
      }
}";

var tree = CSharpSyntaxTree.ParseText(code);

var operators = new List<SyntaxKind>()
{
        SyntaxKind.GreaterThanToken,
        SyntaxKind.GreaterThanEqualsToken,
        SyntaxKind.LessThanEqualsToken,
        SyntaxKind.LessThanToken,
        SyntaxKind.EqualsEqualsToken,
        SyntaxKind.LessThanLessThanEqualsToken,
        SyntaxKind.GreaterThanGreaterThanEqualsToken

};
```

```
tree.GetRoot()
    .DescendantNodes()
        .Where (t => t.Kind() == SyntaxKind.ClassDeclaration)
        .Cast<ClassDeclarationSyntax>()
        .Select (t =>
          new
          {
                  ClassName = t.Identifier.ValueText,//#1
              MethodTokens
                = t.Members
            .Where (m => m.Kind() == SyntaxKind.MethodDeclaration)
.Cast<MethodDeclarationSyntax>()
.Select (
      mds =>
      new
      {
          MethodName = mds.Identifier.ValueText,
            Tokens = CSharpSyntaxTree.ParseText(mds.ToFullString())
                .GetRoot()
                .DescendantTokens()
                .Select(c => c.Kind())
      })
.Select (w =>
  new
  {
    MethodName = w.MethodName, //#2
    Toks = w.Tokens.Zip(w.Tokens.Skip(1),(a,b)=>
                          operators.Any (op => op == a ) && b
          == SyntaxKind.NumericLiteralToken)//#3
  })
.Where (w => w.Toks.Any (to => to == true))//#4
.Select (w => w.MethodName)
}).Dump();
```

That code produces the output shown in Figure 2-9.

Figure 2-9. *Methods that use magic numbers in conditions*

The line marked #1 finds the class declarations from the sample code. Line #2 finds the names of the methods in the class declaration. Line #3 finds all the tokens used in the method body. Line #4 checks if any of the tokens used in the method body is of type NumericLiteralToken or not. This is essentially checking whether a magic number is used in the condtion or not.

Ladder if Statements

Sometimes you find code that calls a particular method over and over again, and the following toy example illustrates such a situation. The function c1() is called multiple times and checked against multiple constant literals. Generally, these types of continuous branching of if statements are called *ladder if statements* because of the structural similarity with ladder.

Ladder if statements can be replaced with carefully crafted rules table modelled as a list of tuples. Listing 2-4 shows how to find methods that use ladder if statements.

Listing 2-4. Finding Methods That Use Ladder if Statements

```
string code =
@"void fun()
{
        //Call a function only once
        if(c1() == 1)
            f1();
        if(c1() == 2)
            f2();
      if(c1() == 3)
         f3();
        if(c1() == 4)
          f4();
        if(co() == 23)
          f22();
        if(co() == 24)
          f21();
}
void funny()
{
    read_that();
    if(c1() == 3)
        c13();
    if(c2() == 34)
        c45();
}
";

var tree = CSharpSyntaxTree.ParseText(code);

tree.GetRoot()
    .DescendantNodes()
        .Where (t => t.Kind() == SyntaxKind.MethodDeclaration)
        .Cast<MethodDeclarationSyntax>()
        .Select (t =>
        new
        {
          Name   = t.Identifier.ValueText,
          IfStatements = t.Body.Statements
            .Where (s => s.Kind() == SyntaxKind.IfStatement)
          .Cast<IfStatementSyntax>()})
```

```
    .Select (t =>
       new
       {
               Name = t.Name,
               Ladders = t.IfStatements
          .Select (i => i.Condition.ToFullString())
   .ToLookup (i => i.Substring(0,i.IndexOf('=')))
   .Where (i => i.Count ()>=2)
   })
    .Dump();
```

The preceding code produces the output shown in Figure 2-10.

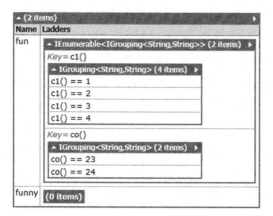

Figure 2-10. *Methods with ladder* if *statements*

This works the same way in which fragmented conditions are found (discussed in the next section).

Fragmented Conditions

Sometimes many if blocks do the same thing if either of many different conditions becomes true. These conditions can be clubbed together using the or operator to combine the logic in a single if statement. But watch out for very big convoluted if statements. You have to somehow strike a balance between the fragmented conditions like the toy example shows here or a very large, complex if statement. However, if the if block becomes too big, you can always extract parts of that complex statement and create smaller methods that will improve the code readability considerably. Listing 2-5 shows how to find methods that fail this test.

Listing 2-5. Finding Methods that Have Fragmented Conditions

```
//Find if statements in each functions where
//they can be clubbed.
string code = @"public class A{int maybe_do_something(...) {
    if(something != -1)
        return 0;
    if(somethingelse != -1)
```

```
        return 0;
    if(etc != -1)
        return 0;
    do_something();
}
int otherFun()
{
    if(bailIfIEqualZero == 0)
  return;
if(string.IsNullOrEmpty(shouldNeverBeEmpty))
  return;

if(betterNotBeNull == null || betterNotBeNull.RunAwayIfTrue)
  return;
    return 1;
}}";

//pull up

var tree = CSharpSyntaxTree.ParseText(code);

tree.GetRoot()
    .DescendantNodes()
        .Where (t => t.Kind() == SyntaxKind.MethodDeclaration)
        .Cast<MethodDeclarationSyntax>()//#1
        .Select (t => new { Name = t.Identifier.ValueText,
                            IfStatements = t.Body.Statements
        .Where (m => m.Kind() == SyntaxKind.IfStatement)
        .Cast<IfStatementSyntax>()
        .Select (iss =>
            //#2
          new {Statement = iss.Statement.ToFullString(),
            //#3
                IfStatement = iss.Condition.ToFullString()})
      //#4
        .ToLookup (iss => iss.Statement)})
        .Dump("Fragmented conditions");
```

The preceding code produces the output shown in Figure 2-11.

Fragmented conditions

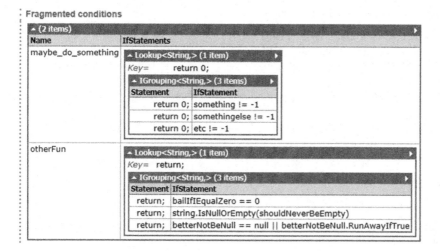

Figure 2-11. *Methods that use fragmented conditions*

Line #1 finds the method declarations from the sample code. Line #2 finds the statements (the actions that get executed should the associated if return true), and line #3 finds the if statements. Line #4 creates a lookup table where the keys represent the statements.

Hungarian Names for Variables

Hungarian notation was started initally to aid programmers in understanding the data type of the variable in a language that didn't have any concept of a data type except a machine word. In the Hungarian naming convention, the first letter of the variable name denotes the type of the variable. For example, consider the lines shown in Figure 2-12.

```
float fIntRate = 4.456;
float intRate = 4.53;
long  liX = 342;
bool bCondi = false;
```

Figure 2-12. *Examples of Hungarian variable names*

In these lines, the first token denotes the type of the variable, and then the first letter of the variable name denotes the type of the variable one more time. Finally, the initialization value makes it clear what could be the type of the variable, although that's not that obvious. These types of variable declarations violates the *don't repeat yourself* (DRY) rule of software engineering.

Listing 2-6 shows how to find such Hungarian notation declarations in variable declarations. The same should be avoided in parameter names in methods and local variable names in methods. The listing shows how to find usage of Hungarian names in the code.

Listing 2-6. Finding Hungarian Names from Source Code

```
//Avoid hungarian notation. It's a code smell now
//refer http://web.mst.edu/~cpp/common/hungarian.html
//applicable to
//class level variables
//temporary variables in methods
//method parameters

string code =
@"class A
 {
    float fIntRate = 4.456;
    float intRate = 4.53;
    long  liX = 342;
    bool bCondi = false;
    string name = ""Sam"";
    string strTitle = ""Mr"";
}";

//#1
Func<string,string,bool> IsHungarian = (varName, typeName) =>
{
    bool result = false;
    string upperCase = "ABCDEFGHIJKLMNOPQRSTUVWXYZ";
    if(typeName == "bool"
  && varName.StartsWith("b")
  && upperCase.Contains(varName[1]))
        result = true;
        if(typeName == "char"
      && varName.StartsWith("c")
      && upperCase.Contains(varName[1]))
            result = true;
        if(typeName == "string"
        && varName.StartsWith("str")
  && upperCase.Contains(varName[1]))
                        result = true;
        if(typeName == "int"
        && varName.StartsWith("i")
        && upperCase.Contains(varName[1]))
                        result = true;
        if(typeName == "float"
      && varName.StartsWith("f")
      && upperCase.Contains(varName[1]))
                        result = true;
        if(typeName == "short"
        && varName.StartsWith("s")
        && upperCase.Contains(varName[1]))
                        result = true;
        if(typeName == "long"
```

```
                && varName.StartsWith("l")
                && upperCase.Contains(varName[1]))
                            result = true;

            return result ;
    };

var tree = CSharpSyntaxTree.ParseText(code);

tree.GetRoot()
    .DescendantNodes()
    .Where (t => t.Kind() == SyntaxKind.FieldDeclaration)
    .Cast<FieldDeclarationSyntax>()
    .Select (fds =>
  new
  {
        //#2
        TypeName = fds.Declaration.Type.ToFullString().Trim(),
        //#3
        VarName = fds.Declaration.Variables
          .Select (v => v.Identifier.Value).First ()
  })
//#4
.Where (fds => IsHungarian(fds.VarName.ToString(),

fds.TypeName.ToString()))
        .Dump("Hungaranian Notations");
```

The preceding code produces the output shown in Figure 2-13.

Hungaranian Notations

▲ (2 items) ▶	
TypeName	**VarName**
float	fIntRate
bool	bCondi

Figure 2-13. *Hungarian names found in the sample code*

The IsHungarian function checks whether a given variable declaration is Hungarian or not. This function is declared near the line in the listing marked #1. Line #2 fills the name of the type of the variable. Line #3 fills the variable name. These two data points will be required by the IsHungarian method to determine whether the variable declaration is Hungarian or not. Line #4 filters the list of variables to find only Hungarian ones.

Lots of Local Variables in Methods

If a method declares lots of local variables, it becomes difficult to reason about the correctness of the code, let alone refactor should the need to do so occur. Local variables should be kept to a minimum, and if a functional style is used, then the need to use local variables will reduce drastically, because most of the time local variables are used to hold the intermediate value of some long calculation.

Listing 2-7 finds the number of local variables used in methods.

Listing 2-7. Finding the Number of Local Variables Used

```
string code  = @"int fun(int x)
                 {
                    int y = 0;
                    x++;
                    return x+1;
                 }
                 double funny(double x)
                 {
                      return x/2.13;
                 }";
SyntaxTree tree = CSharpSyntaxTree.ParseText(code);

List<MethodDeclarationSyntax> methods =
tree.GetRoot()
    .DescendantNodes()
    .Where(d => d.Kind() == SyntaxKind.MethodDeclaration)
    .Cast<MethodDeclarationSyntax>()
    .ToList();//#1

methods
      .Select(z =>
         new { MethodName = z.Identifier.ValueText,//#2
               NBLocal = z.Body.Statements
     //#3
    .Count(x => x.Kind() == SyntaxKind.LocalDeclarationStatement) })
.OrderByDescending(x => x.NBLocal)
.ToList()
.ForEach(x =>
    Console.WriteLine(x.MethodName + " " + x.NBLocal));
```

The listing code produces the output shown in Figure 2-14.

fun 1
funny 0

Figure 2-14. *The number of local variables in methods*

This means that the function has only one local variable declaration, whereas funny doesn't have any. Line #1 finds all the method declarations in the sample code, line #2 finds the name of those methods, and line #3 finds the number of local variables used.

Methods Not Using All Parameters

Source code should be optimal. There shouldn't be anything that is not serving its purpose. So if a method is not using all of its parameters, it's just adding clutter to the source code. This can confuse developers, leaving them under the impression that any of those parameters might be useful. Nobody wants to break a working code, so developers shy away from deleting/getting rid of those parameters.

Listing 2-8 finds methods that don't use all the parameters given to them using Roslyn.

Listing 2-8. Finds Methods that Don't Use All the Parameters

```
string code = @"int fun(int x,int z)
                {
                  int y = 0;
                  x++;
                  return x+1;
                }
                double funny(double x)
                {
                  return x/2.13;
                }";

SyntaxTree tree = CSharpSyntaxTree.ParseText(code);

List<MethodDeclarationSyntax> methods =

tree.GetRoot()
    .DescendantNodes()
    .OfType<MethodDeclarationSyntax>().ToList();

methods.Select(z =>
               {
                   var parameters =
                   z.ParameterList.Parameters
                   .Select(p => p.Identifier.ValueText);
```

```
            return
                  new
                  {
                      MethodName =
                        z.Identifier.ValueText,//#1
                      //#2
                      IsUsingAllParameter =
                      parameters.All
                (x => z.Body.Statements.SelectMany (s => s.DescendantTokens()).Select (s =>
s.ValueText).Distinct().Contains(x))};

})
.Where(x => !x.IsUsingAllParameter)
.ToList()
.ForEach(x => Console.WriteLine(x.MethodName + " "
                    + x.IsUsingAllParameter));
```

The code produces the following output:

```
fun False
```

Line #1 finds the name of methods, and line #2 checks whether the method uses all the parameters that were given to it. The following line of code projects all the distinct token names and checks whether all parameter names are found from that list or not:

```
z.Body.Statements.SelectMany (s => s.DescendantTokens()).Select (s => s.ValueText).
Distinct().Contains(x))
```

Multiple Return Statements

If a method has more than one `return` statement, it becomes difficult to refactor that method should such a need occur. Listing 2-9 finds such multiple `return` statements from methods—it finds all methods that have multiple `return` statements.

Listing 2-9. Finding Methods with Multiple Return Statements

```
string code =
@"int fun(int x)
{
   x++;
   if (x == 0)
      return x
   else
      return x+2;
}
double funny3(int x)
{
  return x/12;
}";

var tree = CSharpSyntaxTree.ParseText(code);
```

```
tree.GetRoot()
.DescendantNodes()
.Where (t => t.Kind() == SyntaxKind.MethodDeclaration)
.Cast<MethodDeclarationSyntax>()
.Select (t =>
 new
 {
   Name = t.Identifier.ValueText, //#1
   Returns = t.Body.DescendantTokens()
        .Count (st => st.Kind() == SyntaxKind.ReturnKeyword)//#2
 })
//Method should ideally have one return statement
//That way it is easier to refactor them later.
.Where (t => t.Returns > 1)                        .Dump("Multiple return
statements");
```

The preceding code produces the output shown in Figure 2-15.

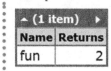

Multiple return statements

Name	Returns
fun	2

Figure 2-15. *Methods with multiple* return *statements*

Line #1 finds the name of the methods in the sample code, and line #2 finds the number of return statements inside the method body.

Long Parameter Lists

A method with a long parameter list is hard to understand. To make things worse, it becomes increasingly difficult for refactoring such methods because it becomes almost impossible to reason about clubbing parameters in an object. Original authors might find it difficult to remember what the parameter was supposed to do, let alone other contributors who came late. There are two reasons this code smells exists: primarily because developers generally have an obsession toward the primitive type (a.k.a *primitive obsession*), and secondarily because lots of legacy code could have been inherited; which heavily relied on interops like COM, which takes several parameters.

Listing 2-10 finds the number of parameters of all methods.

Listing 2-10. Finding the Number of Parameters of All Methods

```
string code =
@"class A
{
   public void f(int a,int b,int c,
        int d,bool x,bool z,float t)
   {
   }
```

```
   public void f3(int a,int b,int c)
   {
   }
}
class B
{
        public void f3b(int a,int b,int c,
                  float d,bool x,bool z,float t)
        {
        }
        public void fb(int a,int b,int c)
        {
        }
}";

var tree = CSharpSyntaxTree.ParseText(code);

tree.GetRoot()
    .DescendantNodes()
        .OfType<ClassDeclarationSyntax>()
        .Select (cds =>
                new
                { ClassName = cds.Identifier.ValueText,//#1

Methods = cds.Members.OfType<MethodDeclarationSyntax>()
 .Select (mds => new {MethodName = mds.Identifier.ValueText//#2
, Parameters = mds.ParameterList.Parameters.Count//#3
})}).Dump();
```

Line #1 finds the classnames from the sample code, line #2 finds the method names, and line #3 finds the number of parameters.

The code produces the output shown in Figure 2-16.

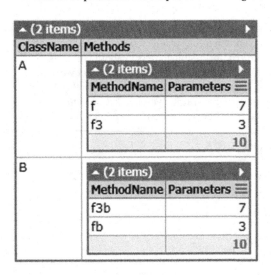

Figure 2-16. *Number of parameters in a method*

goto Labels

goto labels are bad. You have been warned not to use them. I have not used goto in my career, and I have authored all sorts of things, from simple games to fully functional web applications, without ever needing goto. Trust me, you can get by without using this construct. Please don't use it because you have to be extremely sure about what you are going to do.

Listing 2-11 finds methods that use goto.

Listing 2-11. Finding Methods that Use goto Labels

```
//avoid goto
string code = @"class SwitchTest
{
        public static void message()
        {
        }
        public void gotoFun()
        {
        // Search:
        for (int i = 0; i < x; i++)
        {
            for (int j = 0; j < y; j++)
            {
                if (array[i, j].Equals(myNumber))
                {
                    goto Found;
                }
            }
        }
    }
    }
    static void Main()
    {
        Console.WriteLine(@""Coffee sizes: 1=Small 2=Medium
                        3=Large"");
        Console.Write(""Please enter your selection: "");
        string s = Console.ReadLine();
        int n = int.Parse(s);
        int cost = 0;
        switch (n)
        {
            case 1:
                cost += 25;
                break;
            case 2:
                cost += 25;
                goto case 1;
            case 3:
                cost += 50;
                goto case 1;
            default:
```

```
                    Console.WriteLine(""Invalid selection."");
                    break;
        }

        Console.ReadKey();
    }
}";

var tree = CSharpSyntaxTree.ParseText(code);

tree.GetRoot()
    .DescendantNodes()
        .Where (t => t.Kind() == SyntaxKind.ClassDeclaration)
        .Cast<ClassDeclarationSyntax>()
        .Select (cds =>
            new
             {
                ClassName = cds.Identifier.ValueText,
                 Methods =
                cds.Members
                .Where (m => m.Kind() ==
                    SyntaxKind.MethodDeclaration)
                     .Cast<MethodDeclarationSyntax>()
                     .Select (mds =>
                     new
                      {
                          MethodName =    mds.Identifier.ValueText,
                          HasGoto  =
                      CSharpSyntaxTree.ParseText(mds.ToString())
                             .GetRoot()
                                  .DescendantTokens()
        //Checking whether the method uses "goto" labels or not        .Any (st => st.Kind()
== SyntaxKind.GotoKeyword)})

.Where (mds => mds.HasGoto)

.Select (mds => mds.MethodName)})
    .Dump("Classwise methods which use goto");
```

That code produces the output shown in Figure 2-17.

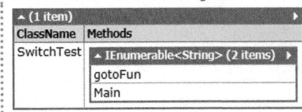

Classwise methods which use goto

ClassName	Methods
SwitchTest	▲ IEnumerable<String> (2 items) ▶
	gotoFun
	Main

Figure 2-17. *Methods using goto labels*

Large Class

A class with lot of methods and members is very hard to comprehend. In general, any class with lots of public methods is very hard to refactor, and it's also very hard to distribute the workload among developers; thus large classes are advised to be avoided. These type of large objects are sometime referred as *God* objects. The code in Listing 2-2 finds large classes—classes that have more methods than their peers on average.

Listing 2-12. Finding Large (God) Classes

```
var code =
          @"class A
              {
                 public int g {get;set;}
                 public void f1(){ }
                 public void f2(){ }
                 public void f3(){ }
                 public void f4(){ }
                 public void f5(){ }
                 public void f6(){ }
              }
          class B
          {
            public void f22(){ }
            public void f32(){ }
          }";

var tree = CSharpSyntaxTree.ParseText(code);

var classAndMembers = tree.GetRoot()
    .DescendantNodes()
        .Where (t => t.Kind() == SyntaxKind.ClassDeclaration)
        .Cast<ClassDeclarationSyntax>()//#1
        .Select (cds =>
      new {ClassName = cds.Identifier.ValueText,//#2
            Size = cds.Members.Count//#3
});

var averageLength =
  classAndMembers
  .Select (classDetails => classDetails.Size)
  .Average ();//#4

classAndMembers
  .Where (am => am.Size > averageLength)//#5
  .Dump("Large Class");
```

The preceding code produces the output shown in Figure 2-18.

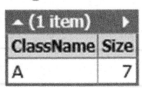

Figure 2-18. *Finding large/God objects*

Line #1 finds all the class declarations in the code, and line #2 finds the name of the class and puts it in the attribute `ClassName`. Line #3 finds the number of members of the class—this number can be thought to be the size of the class. Line #4 finds the average size of classes. Line #5 finds classes whose size is bigger than the average.

Lines of Code

Although the number of lines shouldn't be used to understand how good code is, longer code definitely adds to the maintainability issue. The motto is *If you can get things done with less code, which makes it more readable, then use less code*. Use libraries of the language. Listing 2-13 finds lines of code.

Listing 2-13. Finding Lines of Code per Method

```
string code =
@"class A
{
   void  Test()
   {
     for (int i = 1; i < 101; i++)
     {
         if (i % 3 == 0 && i % 5 == 0)
         {
             Console.WriteLine(""FizzBuzz"");
         }
         //Just a comment
         else if (i % 3 == 0)
         {
             Console.WriteLine(""Fizz"");
         }
         else if (i % 5 == 0)
         {
             Console.WriteLine(""Buzz"");
         }
```

```
            else
            {
                Console.WriteLine(i);
            }
        }
      }


}
class Z
{
        int funny = 1;
        void fun2()
        {
              updateThat();
        }
        void funny2()
        {
              Console.WriteLine(funny);
        }
}";

var tree = CSharpSyntaxTree.ParseText(code);

tree.GetRoot()
    .DescendantNodes()
        .Where (t => t.Kind() == SyntaxKind.ClassDeclaration)
        .Cast<ClassDeclarationSyntax>()
        .Select (cds =>
              new {
                          ClassName = cds.Identifier.ValueText,//#1
                       Methods = cds.Members
                         .OfType<MethodDeclarationSyntax>()
                         .Select (mds =>
                         new {
                    MethodName = mds.Identifier.ValueText,//#2
                       LOC = mds.Body.SyntaxTree
 .GetLineSpan(mds.FullSpan).EndLinePosition.Line //#3
 -  mds.Body.SyntaxTree.GetLineSpan(mds.FullSpan)
          .StartLinePosition.Line -3 //#4
})
}
)
.Dump();
```

The preceding code produces the output shown in Figure 2-19.

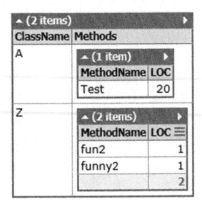

Figure 2-19. *Lines of code per method*

Line #1 finds the class name, and line #2 finds the method name in the current class. Line #3 finds the beginning of the method, and line #4 finds the end of the method. The difference between these two numeric fields returns the number of lines of code in the method. Three is subtracted to account for the method signature and the opening and closing braces.

Control Flags

Controlling logic using a Boolean field that can be updated elsewhere is a bad design idea because it can lead to side effects. The Boolean field is known as a *control flag*. The name *flag* stems from the fact that it can either be set or unset (kind of like a flag that can either be hoisted or not).

Listing 2-14 finds methods in a sample code that uses control flags.

Listing 2-14. Finding Code Lines that Have a Control Flag in a Condition

```
string code =
  @"class BaseClass
    {
        bool cflag  = false;
        void update()
        {
                if(!flag)
                    if(thatThing())
                        flag = true;

        }

        void thatOtherThing()
        {
                bool flag = false;
                if(flag)
              {
                    //Do that
              }
```

```
                        else
                        {
                                //Do something else
                                flag = false;
                        }
                }";
//Find all boolean variables in the class
//Find all if statements that solely rely on those
//Find the methods in which these if statements are

var tree = CSharpSyntaxTree.ParseText(code);

var bools = tree.GetRoot()
    .DescendantNodes()

    .Where (t => t.Kind() == SyntaxKind.VariableDeclaration
&& t.ToFullString().Trim().StartsWith("bool"))

    .Select (t =>
            new
              {
                VariableName = t.ToFullString().Trim()
                                        .Split(' ')[1],
                Class = t.Ancestors()
                            .Where
                (x => x.Kind() == SyntaxKind.ClassDeclaration)
             .Cast<ClassDeclarationSyntax>()
             .First().Identifier.ValueText})
          .Select (t => t.VariableName);//#1

tree.GetRoot()
        .DescendantNodes()
        .Where (t => t.Kind == SyntaxKind.IfStatement)
        .Cast<IfStatementSyntax>()
        .Select (ifs =>

                new
                  {
                    If = ifs.ToFullString(), //#2
                    Condition = ifs.Condition.ToFullString(),//#3
                    Line = ifs.SyntaxTree
                                .GetLineSpan(ifs.FullSpan,false)
                                .StartLinePosition.Line+1//#4
                  })
        .Where (ifs => ifs.Condition.Split(new string[]{"&&", "||", "==","(",")"," "
"},StringSplitOptions.RemoveEmptyEntries)
        //If a control flag is used,
        .Any (c => bools.Contains(c) ||
        //it can also be used in a negative way. skipping "!"
                bools.Contains(c.Substring(1))))//#5

.Dump("if nodes with control flags");
```

The preceding code produces the output shown in Figure 2-20.

if nodes with control flags

▲ (2 items)			▶
If	**Condition**	**Line** ≡	

if(!flag)
if(thatThing())
flag = true;
	!flag	6	

if(flag)
{
  //Do that
}
else
{
  //Do something else
  flag = false;
}
	flag	15	

		21	

Figure 2-20. *Control flag usages in conditions*

Line #1 finds all the Boolean variables that are declared at class level. Line #2 puts the entire `if` statement in the attribute `if`. Line #3 puts the condition of each `if` statement in the attribute `Condition`. Line #4 gets the line number of this statement. Line #5 checks whether the condition of the `if` block solely comprises of only one Boolean variable or not. If it does comprise of only one Boolean variable, then the condition is using a control flag.

Code-to-Comment Ratio

Code that's well written doesn't require much comment to go along with it. A very low *code-to-comment* ratio can be a signal of a bad algorithm implementation. This can be thought of as similar to a signal-to-noise (SNR) ratio. A high SNR ratio is indicator of good design in electrical engineering. Low SNR is an indicator of a bad design. Similarly a high code-to-comment ratio is a great sign of good easy-to-understand code. The reverse indicates a situation to be avoided. Listing 2-15 finds code-to-comment ratio in all classes in a given source code.

Listing 2-15. Finding Code-to-Comment Ratio Classes and Methods

```
string code =
@"class A
 {
     int fun(int x)
     {
         //update x
         x++;
         return x - 3;
     }
     int add(int x,int y)
```

```
            {
                //add these two
                //it might lead to exception
                 return x + y;
              }
    }
}
class B
{
    int fun3(int x)
    {
         //update x
         x++;
         return x - 3;
    }
    int add2(int x,int y)
    {
        //add these two
        //it might lead to exception
        return x + y;
    }
}";

var tree = CSharpSyntaxTree.ParseText(code);

tree.GetRoot()
    .DescendantNodes()
        .Where (t => t.Kind() == SyntaxKind.ClassDeclaration)
        .Cast<ClassDeclarationSyntax>()
        .Select (t =>
            new
              {
                 ClassName = t.Identifier.ValueText,
                  Methods =
                 t.Members.OfType<MethodDeclarationSyntax>()
              })//#1
        .Select (t =>
            new {ClassName = t.ClassName,
                      MethodDetails = t.Methods
           .Select (m => new { Name = m.Identifier.ValueText,
             Lines = m.Body.Statements.Count, //#2
             Comments = m.Body.DescendantTrivia()
                                  .Count (b => b.Kind() ==
                SyntaxKind.SingleLineCommentTrivia
    ||  b.Kind == SyntaxKind.MultiLineCommentTrivia) //#3
})})

        .Dump("Code and Comment per method per class");
```

That code produces the output shown in Figure 2-21.

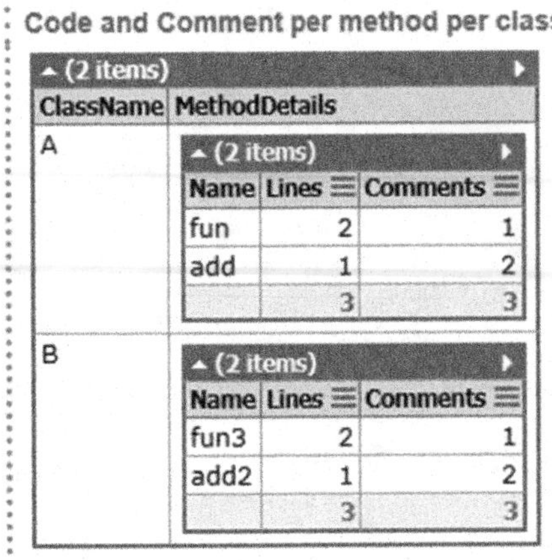

Code and Comment per method per class

ClassName	MethodDetails		
A	**Name**	**Lines**	**Comments**
	fun	2	1
	add	1	2
		3	3
B	**Name**	**Lines**	**Comments**
	fun3	2	1
	add2	1	2
		3	3

Figure 2-21. *Code-to-comment ratio for classes/methods*

Line #1 generates a collection with the name of the class and the methods in that class. Line #2 calculates the number of code lines (source code) in each method. Line #3 calculates the number of comments in each method.

Summary

Congratulations on finishing a really large chapter! I hope you enjoyed the journey. In this chapter you learned how Roslyn and LINQ can be used to extract several metrics to understand code health. In the next chapter you will see how Roslyn can be used to detect problems in software design. Then you'll see how Roslyn and LINQ can be used to detect patterns in code, and later in the book how programmers can be identified from their source code.

CHAPTER 3

Design Quality Metrics

When a house is built, the engineer first builds its plan and then a model. Once all the stakeholders are satisfied with the model, then they go about constructing the actual house. However, in the software industry, design is neglected. It may seem that the cost of a design alteration in software is not much, but it is enormous. It acts as a butterfly effect. Catching bad design choices early is every architect's dream. But it doesn't happen with software, for several reasons. First, once the design choices are described and laid out, several developers start to implement the design, much as workers keep working to make a house. However unlike working on a house, software developers check in their code after a code review. No design review happens beforehand—it's unclear what the design review expectations would be. So, developers check in code that may work but that may be far outside the design choices made initially. Thus over time, as the codebase grows bigger and bigger, the design deviates from one part of the product to the other. If the overall code were compared to a huge castle, the architecture from one part of the castle to the next would be very different.

In this chapter you shall see how some of the signals of bad design choices can be caught using Roslyn. I hope you pick up on the general idea about how to code up for your specific design choices. Using the techniques in this chapter, you can set up an automated design review.

Each of the following sections describes a design problem or a symptom that can signal a bad design choice followed by a Roslyn/LINQ/C# script to catch these.

Deeply Nested Loops

Nested loops are one of the main reasons for slow software. In general, any nesting beyond three levels deep is a strict no-no and a sign that you should look for to identify very bad design early on. Rosly makes it possible to look for nested loops, as shown in Listing 3-1.

Listing 3-1. Roslyn Code to Find Deeply Nested Loops

```
string code =
@"//The following code snippet contains
  //few very deeply nested looping constructs
  //that are generally advised to avoid.
  void fun2(int x)
  {
      for (int i =0;i<10;i++)
    {
        for (int j = 0;j<10;j++)
              list.Add(i+j);
    }
  }
```

```
   void fun(int x)
   {
        for (int i =0;i<10;i++)
        {
            for (int j = 0;j<10;j++)
            {
                for(int k = 2;k<20;k++)
                            list.Add(i+j+k);
            }
        }
}
   void straightLoop()
   {
                for(int j = 0; j< 10; j++)
                        doThat(j);
   }
   void loopingTheLoopWhile()
   {
                while(true)
                        for(int x = 0;x<10;x++)
                                foreach(var z in z[x])
                                        doSome(z);
   }
   void loopingTheLoop()
   {
        foreach(var m in newItems)
                foreach(var z in oldItems)
                        for(int i = 0;  i< z.Items.Count;i++)
                                    doThat(i,z,m);
   }
   void fun4(int x)
   {
        for(int m = 0;m<10;m+=2)
                for (int i =0;i<10;i++)
                {
                    for (int j = 0;j<10;j++)
                    {
                        for(int k = 2;k<20;k++)
                                    list.Add(i+j+k);
                    }
                }
   }";

var tree = CSharpSyntaxTree.ParseText(code);//#1
var loopTypes = new List<SyntaxKind>()
{
        SyntaxKind.ForStatement,
        SyntaxKind.ForEachStatement,
        SyntaxKind.WhileStatement
};//#2
tree.GetRoot()
```

46

```
        .DescendantNodes()
        .Where(t => loopTypes.Any(l => t.Kind() == l))//#3
        .Select(t => new
        {
                //#4
Method = t.Ancestors().OfType<MethodDeclarationSyntax>()
.First()
.Identifier.ValueText,
                Nesting = 1 + t.Ancestors()
.Count(z => loopTypes
.Any(l => z.Kind() == l))
        })//#5
        .ToLookup(t => t.Method)
        .ToDictionary(t => t.Key,
                t => t.Select(m => m.Nesting).Max())//#6
        .Select(t => new { Method = t.Key, Nesting = t.Value})
        .Where(t => t.Nesting >= 3)//#7
        .Dump("Deeply Nested Loops");
```

The preceding code produces the output shown in Figure 3-1.

Deeply Nested Loops

▲ (4 items) ▶	
Method	**Nesting ☰**
fun	3
loopingTheLoopWhile	3
loopingTheLoop	3
fun4	4
	13

Figure 3-1. *Showing nesting level of loops*

The code line marked #1 parses the source code to get the C# syntax tree. Line #2 creates a list representing different kind of loops. Line #3 filters the code to find any kind of nesting of loops inside other/similar type of loops. At line #4 a projection is created such that each method name and the nesting level of the loop inside those are projected. Line # 5 creates a lookup based on the method name such that the maximum nesting level for loops for each method is projected in line #6 in a dictionary, where *keys* represent the name of the methods and *values* represent the maximum level of nesting depth. Line #7 filters out okish loops and leaves the really deep ones to be reported. A loop nesting level more than three levels deep is really bad idea, although unavoidable in some situations. But this script will help you find the avoidable nested loops that will cause potential performance issues if left unaddressed.

Out Parameters

out parameters can lead to disastrous situations as they can update the state of a variable without getting noticed. The script in Listing 3-2 finds the defaulter methods that use out parameters. In my career of over a decade of programming, I can't remember when I have used one.

47

Listing 3-2. Roslyn Code to Find Methods with out Parameters

```
//avoid out parameter
string code = @"class OutExample
{
    static void Method(out int i)
    {
        i = 44;
    }
    static void Main()
    {
        int value;
        Method(out value);
        // value is now 44
    }
}";

var tree = CSharpSyntaxTree.ParseText(code);

tree.GetRoot()
    .DescendantNodes()
        .OfType<ClassDeclarationSyntax>()//#1
        .Select(cds => new
        {
                ClassName = cds.Identifier.ValueText,
                Methods = cds.Members
                        .OfType<MethodDeclarationSyntax>()//#2
                  .Where(mds => //#3
                     mds.ParameterList
                        .Parameters.Any(z =>
                                  z.Modifiers.Any(m =>
                           m.ValueText == "out")))
                        .Select(mds => mds.Identifier.ValueText)
        })
.Dump("Methods with \"out\" parameters");
```

The preceding code produces the output shown in Figure 3-2.

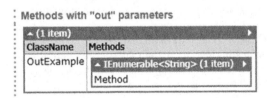

Figure 3-2. *Output of* out *parameter finder*

Line #1 finds all the class declarations from the given code. Then in line #2, all methods of all classes are found. The filter clause Where at line #3 finds only those methods that have at least one parameter marked as out in their parameter list.

Deeply Nested if Blocks (Bow and Arrow)

Nested if statements are one of the main reasons software can be difficult to understand, and they also add to redundant lines of code. For example, consider the source code shown in Figure 3-3.

```
if (x > 20)
    if ( y < 2)
        if( z > 3)
            doThat();
```

Figure 3-3. *Bow and arrow pattern*

As you can see, there is no fall thorough sections for any of the if statements, so essentially there is no need to for this nesting, and all the conditions for the entire set of if statements can be written together in a single line, as shown in Figure 3-4.

```
if (x > 20 &&  y < 2 && z > 3)
                    doThat();
```

Figure 3-4. *Effect of clubbing if statements*

The code snippet in Listing 3-3 shows how to find such set of if statements in the code.

Listing 3-3. Script to Find All the Deeply Nested if Blocks

```
string code =

@"void check(int x)
  {
        if(x<10)
                doSomeThing();
  }
void fun2(int x,int y)
{
if(x<y)
        if(x+y<20)
        doThat();
}
void fun(int x)
{
        //really stupid example
        //but you shall get the point
        int x = 20;
        //Nesting Level 1
        if(x < 10)
        {
                //Nesting Level 2
                if(x - 1 < 10)
                {
```

49

```
                        if( x - 2 < 10)//Nesting Level 3
                        {
                                if (x - 4 < 10)//Nesting Level 4
                                        doThat();
                                else
                                        doOther();
                        }
                }
        }
}";

var tree = CSharpSyntaxTree.ParseText(code);//#1
var loopTypes = new List<SyntaxKind>()
{
        SyntaxKind.IfStatement
};//#2
tree.GetRoot()
        .DescendantNodes()
        .Where(t => loopTypes.Any(l => t.Kind() == l))//#3
        .Select(t => new //#4
        {
                Method =  t.Ancestors()
                        .OfType<MethodDeclarationSyntax>()
                        .First()
                        .Identifier.ValueText,
                Nesting = 1 + t.Ancestors()
                        .Count(z => loopTypes
                            .Any(l => z.Kind() == l))
        })
        .ToLookup(t => t.Method)
        //#5
        .ToDictionary(t => t.Key,
                    t => t.Select(m => m.Nesting).Max())
        .Select(t => new { Method = t.Key, Nesting = t.Value })
        //Find only if blocks that are deeper than 3 levels.
        .Where(t => t.Nesting >= 3)//#6
        .Dump("Deeply nested if-statements");
```

That code produces the output shown in Figure 3-5.

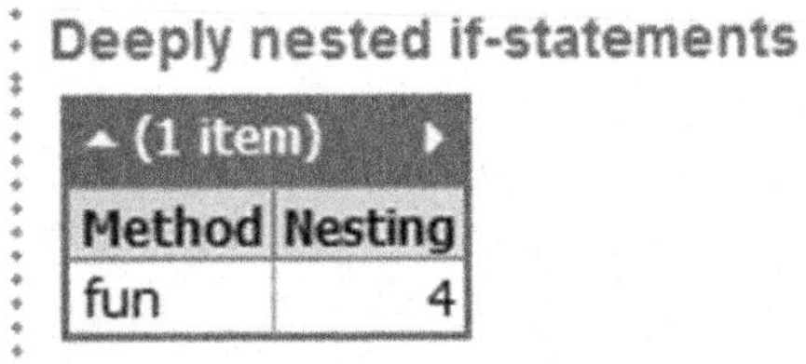

Method	Nesting
fun	4

Figure 3-5. *Result of deeply nested if blocks*

This one works the same way as the previous one. In this case, instead of looping constructs, the nesting finds nested if blocks.

Long List of Switches

A big list of switch case labels is a sign of an antipattern. Mostly a long list of switches can be replaced with polymorphism. Listing 3-4 shows how to find long list of switches using Roslyn and LINQ.

Listing 3-4. Script to Find Long List of Switches

```
string code =
@"public void fun(int a)
{
switch(a)
    {
        case 1:print(1);break;case 2:print(5);break;
        case 3:print(4);break;case 4:print(2);break;
        case 5:print(8);break;case 6:print(7);break;
        case 7:print(7);break;default:print(nothing);break;
}
}
public void fun2(int a)
{
switch(a+1)
{
        case 1:dothat();break;case 2:dothese();break;
}
switch(g)
{
        case 1:print(1);break;case 2:print(5);break;
        case 3:print(4);break;case 4:print(2);break;
        case 5:print(8);break;case 6:print(7);break;
        case 7:print(7);break;default:print(nothing);break;
}
}";//long switch cases

var tree = CSharpSyntaxTree.ParseText(code);//#1
tree.GetRoot()
        .DescendantNodes()
        .OfType<MethodDeclarationSyntax>() //#2
        .Select(mds => //#3
            new
            {
                    Name = mds.Identifier.ValueText,
                    Switches = mds.Body
                            .DescendantNodes()
                                .OfType<SwitchStatementSyntax>()
                    .Select(st =>
                            new
                    {
                        SwitchStatement = st.ToFullString(),
```

51

```
                    //How many switch sections are there
                    //in the switch statement.
                        Sections = st.Sections.Count
                })
                .OrderByDescending(st => st.Sections)//#4
})

.Dump("Switch statements per functions");
```

The preceding code produces the output shown in Figure 3-6.

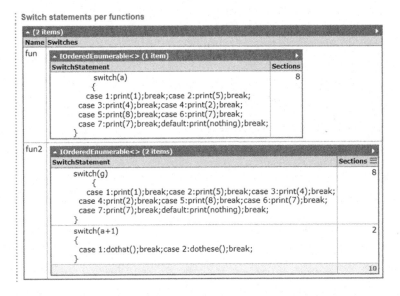

Figure 3-6. *Showing long list of switches*

This code works the same way in which the previous scripts found nested loops and nested if blocks.

Data Classes (That Aren't Classes)

If a class just has a set of public properties and no methods, then that class is called a *data class*. A data class is a code smell that should be avoided, because frankly, it's not a class. It is just data wrapped in a class.

The code in Listing 3-5 finds data classes from source code.

Listing 3-5. Script to Find Data Classes

```
string code =
@"class A
{
        void fun(){}
        void fun1(int a){}
        void fun2(int a, int a){}
```

```
        public int Age {get;set;}
        public string Name {get;set;}
}
//B is a data class smell as it has only public data
class B
{
        public int Age {get;set;}
        public string Name {get;set;}
}

//C is also a data class smell as it has only public data
class C
{
        public double RateOfInterest {get;set;}
}";

var tree = CSharpSyntaxTree.ParseText(code);

var classes = tree
                .GetRoot()
                .DescendantNodes()
                .OfType<ClassDeclarationSyntax>()//#1
                .Select(cds => new //#2
                {
                    //Name of the class
                    Name = cds.Identifier.ValueText,
                    //Number of members of the class
                    MemberCount = cds.Members.Count,
                    //Number of public properties
                    PublicPropertyCount = cds.Members
                .OfType<PropertyDeclarationSyntax>()
                    .Count(pds => pds.Modifiers
                        .Any(m => m.ValueText == "public"))
                })
  .Where(cds => cds.MemberCount == cds.PublicPropertyCount)//#3
  .Dump("Data Classes");
```

That code produces the output shown in Figure 3-7.

Name	MemberCount	PublicPropertyCount
B	2	2
C	1	1
	3	3

Figure 3-7. *Data classes in the sample code*

Line #1 finds classes from the sample code. Line #2 creates a projection with the names of the classes, number of members they have, and number of public properties they have. Line #3 filters out everything except classes where the number of public properties matches that of the total number of members. This results in a display of just the data classes, as shown in Figure 3-7.

Local Classes

Consider using composition when you find yourself requiring a local class. It is not a good practice to have local classes because there are two major concerns. First, local classes can't be shared, and these break the single responsibility principle. Moreover local classes add to the conceptual load of the class. Listing 3-6 uses Roslyn and LINQ to find local classes from several classes in the program.

Listing 3-6. Script to Find Local Classes

```
string code = //Here is a toy sample code
@"class A
{
        //Bad to have local classes.
        class localA
        {

        }
}
class B
{
        void fun()
        {
        }
}
class C
{
        void funny()
        {
        }
}";

var tree = CSharpSyntaxTree.ParseText(code);

tree
.GetRoot()
.DescendantNodes()
.OfType<ClassDeclarationSyntax>()//#1
.Select (cds =>
    new
{
        ClassName = cds.Identifier.ValueText,
        LocalClasses = cds.Members
                        .OfType<ClassDeclarationSyntax>()
                        .Select (m => m.Identifier.ValueText)}
)
.Where (cds => cds.LocalClasses.Count() >= 1)//#3
.Dump("Local Classes");
```

The preceding code produces the output shown in Figure 3-8.

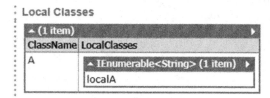

Figure 3-8. *Finding local classes*

Line #1 finds all the classes in the sample code. Line #2 finds all the nested class definitions inside each of the classes. If a class declares a local class, there will be nested class definition syntaxes as one of its members. Line #3 finds all such classes that have at least one local class declaration.

Refused Bequest

Refused bequest is an immediate harmful side effect of using *inheritance*. If a class does not implement most or all methods of an interface that it claims to be inheriting from, then the situation is called a *refused bequest*. The name originates from the fact that this situation is as if the class is refusing the gift given to it. The Roslyn script in Listing 3-7 identifies a probable refused bequest relationship between an interface and a class. This can be easily tweaked to make it work for abstract classes too.

Listing 3-7. Script to Find Possible Cases of Refused Bequest

```
string code =
@"interface ISomething
{
        public void f1();
        public void f2();
}
interface ISomeOtherThing
{
        public void other1();
        public void other2();
}
class A:ISomething,ISomeOtherThing
{
        public void other1()
        {
        }
        public void other2()
        {
        }
        public void f1()
        {
                throw new NotImplementedException();
        }
```

```
        public void f2()
        {
                throw new NotImplementedException();
        }
}
class B:ISomething
{
        int f_1 = 0;
        int f_2 = 1;
        public void f1()
        {
                Console.WriteLine(f_1);
        }
        public void f2()
        {
                Console.WriteLine(f_2);
        }
}";

var tree = CSharpSyntaxTree.ParseText(code);
var interfaces = tree.GetRoot()
                    .DescendantNodes()
                        .OfType<InterfaceDeclarationSyntax>()
                        .Select (ids =>
new
{
        InterfaceName =  ids.Identifier.ValueText,
        MethodNames = ids.Members
                    .OfType<MethodDeclarationSyntax>()
                    .Select(mds  =>  mds.Identifier.ValueText)
})
.ToLookup (ids  =>  ids.InterfaceName,
            ids  =>  ids.MethodNames)
.ToDictionary(ids  =>  ids.Key,
            ids  =>  ids.SelectMany (i  =>  i)

.ToList());//#1

string[] notImpl = {"throw","new","NotImplementedException"};

var result = tree.GetRoot()
            .DescendantNodes()

        .OfType<ClassDeclarationSyntax>()

        .Select (cds  =>
new {
ClassName = cds.Identifier.ValueText,//#2
//get rid of the initial colon
```

```
DerivingFrom = cds.BaseList.GetText()//#3
.ToString()
                .Substring(1)
.Split(new char[]{','},
StringSplitOptions.RemoveEmptyEntries),
Methods = cds.Members
        .OfType<MethodDeclarationSyntax>()
        .Where (mds  =>  mds.Body.Statements.Count == 1)//#4
        .Select (mds  =>
new {
MethodName = mds.Identifier.ValueText,
BelongsTo = interfaces.FirstOrDefault //#5
(i  =>  i.Value.Contains(mds.Identifier.ValueText)), NotImple = mds.Body.Statements[0].
ToFullString()
.Trim()
.Split(new char[]{' ','('},
StringSplitOptions.RemoveEmptyEntries)
        .Take(3)
      .SequenceEqual(new    string[]{"throw","new","NotImplementedException"}
)//#6
})
.Where (mds  =>  mds.BelongsTo.Key != null
&& mds.NotImple )
.Select (mds  =>
new {
MethodName = mds.MethodName,
BelongsTo = mds.BelongsTo.Key,
NotImple = mds.NotImple})})

.Where (cds  =>  cds.Methods.Count () > 0);

result
        .SelectMany (r  =>  r.Methods
        .Select (m  =>   new
                KeyValuePair<string,string>
                (
                        r.ClassName,
                        m.BelongsTo
                )))
        .ToLookup (r  =>  r.Value, r  =>  r.Key)
        .ToDictionary (r  =>  r.Key, r  =>  r
        .Distinct()
        .ToList())
    //#7
        .Select (r  =>  new {InterfaceName = r.Key,
ClassNames = r.Value})
.Dump("Probable Refused Bequest Relationships");
```

57

The preceding code produces the output shown in Figure 3-9.

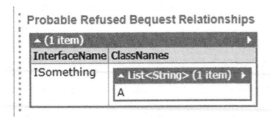

Figure 3-9. *Extracted refused bequest relationship*

Line #1 finds all the interfaces and all the methods that are declared in them and creates a dictionary where the keys represent the names of the interfaces. Line #2 puts the name of the class, and line #3 puts the list of interfaces and classes the class inherit from. Line #4 finds all the methods that have only one line. Methods with only one line are interesting because methods that are not implemented also have only one line body. The body of a non-implemented interface method is as follows:

```
throw new NotImplementedException();
```

Line# 5 finds the interface to which this current method belongs. Line #6 checks whether the class provided a concrete implementation of the method or not.

Finally, line #7 presents the output indexed by interface names—meaning it shows the result of refused bequest relationships between an interface and all other classes. As in the toy example, class A doesn't implement interface methods f1 and f2 from the interface Isomething, and that's why these two entities (class A and interface ISomething) share a refused bequest relationship.

Lots of Overloaded Versions of a Method

Overloading of methods should be kept to a minimum. It can be very confusing if not impossible to figure out—even with named arguments that the 50th verity of an overloaded method is being called out of 60 overloaded versions that differ a little bit in data types or number of parameters. Listing 3-8 finds the number of overloaded methods in each class.

Listing 3-8. Script to Find Number of Overloaded Methods

```
string code = @"class DocumentHome {


  (...)
  public Document createDocument(String name) {
    // just calls another method with default value
    // of its parameter
    return createDocument(name, -1);
  }

  public Document createDocument(String name, i
nt minPagesCount) {
```

```
// just calls another method with default value of its parameter
   return createDocument(name, minPagesCount, false);
 }

 public Document createDocument(String name, int minPagesCount, boolean firstPageBlank) {
   // just calls another method with default value of its parameter
   return createDocument(name, minPagesCount, false, "");
 }

 public Document createDocument(String name, int minPagesCount, boolean firstPageBlank,
String title) {
   // here the real work gets done
   (...)
 }

 (...)
}";

var tree = SyntaxTree.ParseText(code);
tree.GetRoot()
    .DescendantNodes()
        .Where (t => t.Kind == SyntaxKind.ClassDeclaration)
        .Cast<ClassDeclarationSyntax>()
        .Select (cds =>
         new
         {
               ClassName = cds.Identifier.ValueText,//#1
               Methods = cds.Members                            .OfType<MethodDeclarationSy
ntax>()//#2
         .Select (mds => mds.Identifier.ValueText)
       })
        .Select (cds => new { ClassName = cds.ClassName,
                              Overloads = cds.Methods
.ToLookup (m => m)
.ToDictionary (m => m.Key, m => m.Count ())})//#3
.Dump("Overloaded Methods");
```

This produces the output shown in Figure 3-10.

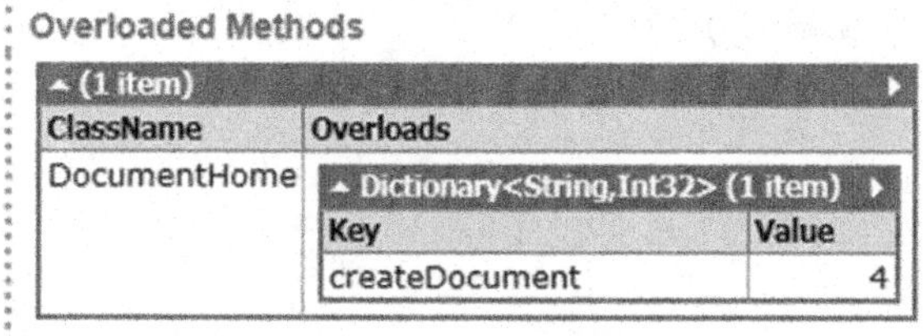

ClassName	Overloads	
DocumentHome	▲ Dictionary<String,Int32> (1 item) ▶	
	Key	Value
	createDocument	4

Figure 3-10. *Finding the number of overloaded methods*

Line #1 gets the name of the class. Line #2 gets the names of all the methods in the current class. Line #3 calculates the number of overloads by generating a lookup table followed by a dictionary where the keys represent the name of the method and the values represent the number of overloads.

Empty Interfaces

Empty interfaces are most often accidental. No one writes an interface that doesn't have any method. The very cause of their existence is accidental. Maybe some time ago the interface was needed and the method in it made sense, but it doesn't make any sense anymore and somebody decided to remove the method it had, because no other types implemented it. That can leave a lasting bad effect on the source code because people (read developers) can get confused. Finding such nuisances is really important. Listing 3-9 helps find such empty interfaces.

Listing 3-9. Script to Find Empty Interfaces

```
string code = @"using System;

namespace DesignLibrary
{
    public interface IGoodInterface
    {
        void funny();
    }
    public interface IBadInterface   // Violates rule
    {
    }
}";

var tree = CSharpSyntaxTree.ParseText(code);

tree.GetRoot()
    .DescendantNodes()
        .OfType<InterfaceDeclarationSyntax>()//#1
        .Select(ids =>   //#2
                    new
                    {
                            InterfaceName = ids.Identifier.ValueText,
                            IsEmpty = ids.Members.Count == 0
                    })
        .Where( thisInterface  => thisInterface.IsEmpty)//#3
        .Dump("Empty Interfaces");
```

The preceding code produces the output shown in Figure 3-11.

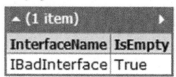

Figure 3-11. *Empty interafaces in the sample code*

Line #1 finds all interfaces in the sample code. Line #2 creates a projection with the names of the interfaces and a Boolean flag indicating whether the interface is empty or not. Line #3 filters out all other interfaces except the empty ones.

Too Many Parameters on Generic Types

Sometimes developers misuse generics. Remember that *generics* is not a way to replace method overloading. Generics only make sense when there is a proper inheritance relationship established either through the is-a class relationship, or by implementing interfaces. It is advisable to avoid excessive parameters on generic types. In fact, anything beyond two generic parameters is considered bad. And trust me, if you design your domain model appropriately, you would never need more than that. Listing 3-10 finds all generic types that use more than two parameters.

Listing 3-10. Finding Generic Types with Excessive Parameters

```
string code = @"private static T FromString<T>(string s) where T : struct
{
    if (typeof(T).Equals(typeof(decimal)))
    {
        var x = (decimal)System.Convert.ToInt32(s) / 100;
        return (T)Convert.ChangeType(x, typeof(T));
    }
    if (typeof(T).Equals(typeof(int)))
    {
        var x = System.Convert.ToInt32(s);
        return (T)Convert.ChangeType(x, typeof(T));
    }
    if (typeof(T).Equals(typeof(DateTime)))
        ... etc ...
}
public string name()
{
        return string.Empty;
}
```

```
//really a bad idea. Trust me!
 private static T FromString2<T,T,T>(string s) where T : struct
{
    if (typeof(T).Equals(typeof(decimal)))
    {
        var x = (decimal)System.Convert.ToInt32(s) / 100;
        return (T)Convert.ChangeType(x, typeof(T));
    }
    if (typeof(T).Equals(typeof(int)))
    {
        var x = System.Convert.ToInt32(s);
        return (T)Convert.ChangeType(x, typeof(T));
    }
    if (typeof(T).Equals(typeof(DateTime)))
        ... etc ...
}";

var tree = CSharpSyntaxTree.ParseText(code);

tree.GetRoot()
    .DescendantNodes()
.OfType<MethodDeclarationSyntax>()
.Select(mds => new { Name = mds.Identifier.ValueText,
Arity = mds.Arity} )
.Where(mds => mds.Arity > 2 )
.Dump("Generic Methods with lots of generic attribute");
```

The preceding code produces the output shown in Figure 3-12.

Generic Methods with lots of generic attribute

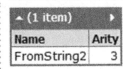

Figure 3-12. *Generic type with more than two parameters*

The number of parameters passed to a generic type is called *arity*. If arity is more than two, then those are the defaulter generic types.

Static Members on Generic Types

As per MSDN

When a static member of a generic type is called, the type argument must be specified for the type. When a generic instance member that does not support inference is called, the type argument must be specified for the member. The syntax for specifying the type argument in these two cases is different and easily confused, as the following calls demonstrate:

```
// Static method in a generic type.
GenericType<int>.StaticMethod();

// Generic instance method that does not support inference.
someObject.GenericMethod<int>();
```

Generally, both of the prior declarations should be avoided so that the type argument does not have to be specified when the member is called. This results in a syntax for calling members in generics that is no different from the syntax for non-generics.

Listing 3-11 shows how to find such types.

Listing 3-11. Script to Find Generic Types with Static Methods

```
var code =
@"class A<T>
{
        public static int fun()
        {
                return 10;
        }

        public int funny<T>()
        {
                return 0;
        }
}";

var tree = CSharpSyntaxTree.ParseText(code);

tree.GetRoot()
    .DescendantNodes()
.OfType<ClassDeclarationSyntax>()
    .Where(cds => cds.Arity > 0)//#1
.Select(cds => //#2

new
        {
        //Name of the generic class
         GenericClassName  = cds.Identifier.ValueText,
        //Static methods in the generic class
        StaticMethods = cds.Members
          .OfType<MethodDeclarationSyntax>()
           .Where(mds => mds.Modifiers
```

```
      .Any(m => m.ValueText == "static"))
      .Select(mds => mds.Identifier.ValueText)
})
.Where(cds => cds.StaticMethods.Count()>0)//#3
.Dump("Static methods on generic types");
```

The preceding code produces the output shown in Figure 3-13.

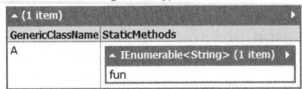

Figure 3-13. *Static methods on generic types*

Line #1 finds all the generic types. A type with arity greater than zero is generic. Line #2 creates a projection with class names and static methods that they have. Line #3 filters out all other generic types except ones that have at least one static method.

Abstract Types with Constructors

Abstract classes shouldn't have constructors. Listing 3-12 finds abstract types that have public constructors.

Listing 3-12. Script to Find Abstract Types with Public Constructors

```
string code = @"using System;


namespace DesignLibrary
{
    public abstract class BadAbstractClassWithConstructor
    {
        // Violates rule: AbstractTypesShouldNotHaveConstructors.
        public BadAbstractClassWithConstructor()
        {
        // Add constructor logic here.
        }
        public abstract void fun(){}
    }
```

```
    public abstract class GoodAbstractClassWithConstructor
    {
        protected GoodAbstractClassWithConstructor()
        {
            // Add constructor logic here.
        }
    }
}
";

var tree = CSharpSyntaxTree.ParseText(code);

var abstractTypes =
tree.GetRoot()
    .DescendantNodes()
    .OfType<ClassDeclarationSyntax>()
    .Where(cds => cds.Modifiers
                        .Any(m => m.ValueText == "abstract"))//#1
    .Select(cds => new //#2
     {

        ClassName = cds.Identifier.ValueText,
         PublicConstructors =
                 cds.Members
                .OfType<ConstructorDeclarationSyntax>()
                                    .Any(c => c.Modifiers
                .Any(m => m.ValueText == "public"))
        })
.Where(cds => cds.PublicConstructors )//#3
.Dump("AbstractTypesShouldNotHaveConstructors Violators");
```

The preceding produces the output shown in Figure 3-14.

AbstractTypesShouldNotHaveConstructors Violators

▲ (1 item)	►
ClassName	**PublicConstructors**
BadAbstractClassWithConstructor	True

Figure 3-14. *Abstract types with public constructors*

Line #1 finds all the abstract classes. Line #2 creates a projection with the name of the class and a Boolean flag indicating whether the type has any public constructor or not. Line #3 filters out every other abstract class except the defaulter ones that has at least one public constructor.

Sealed Class and Protected Members

Sealed classes shouldn't have protected members. As per MSDN

Types declare protected members so that inheriting types can access or override the member. By definition, you cannot inherit from a sealed type, which means that protected methods on sealed types cannot be called. The C# compiler issues a warning for this error.

Listing 3-13 shows how to find such defaulter types.

Listing 3-13. Script to Find Sealed Types with Protected Members

```
var code = @"using System;

namespace DesignLibrary
{
    public sealed class SealedClass
    {
        protected void ProtectedMethod(){}
    }
}";

var tree = CSharpSyntaxTree.ParseText(code);

tree.GetRoot()
    .DescendantNodes()
        .OfType<ClassDeclarationSyntax>()
        .Where(cds => cds.Modifiers
            .Any(m => m.ValueText == "sealed")) //#1
        .Select
        (
                cds => //#2
                new
                {
                        ClassName = cds.Identifier.ValueText,
                        ProtectedMembers =
                                cds.Members
                                .OfType<MethodDeclarationSyntax>()
                                .Where(mds =>
                                mds.Modifiers
                                .Any(m => m.ValueText ==
                                        "protected"))
                                .Select(mds => mds.Identifier
                                        .ValueText)
                }
        )
        .Where(cds => cds.ProtectedMembers.Count() > 0)//#3
        .Dump("CA1047 Defaulters");
```

The preceding code produces the output shown in Figure 3-15. Line #1 finds all the sealed classes. Line #2 creates a projection with the names of the classes and the list of protected members they have. Line #3 finds only those sealed classes that have at least one protected member. Modifiers denote the access modifiers that are used in C# or any other language.

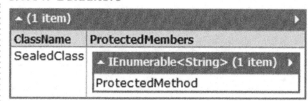

CA1047 Defaulters

ClassName	ProtectedMembers
SealedClass	▲ IEnumerable<String> (1 item) ▶
	ProtectedMethod

Figure 3-15. *Sealed classes with protected members*

Object Obsession

C# is a statically typed language. However, since the base type is object, sometimes developers take that for granted and pass anything and cast it back in the called method. That's bad practice. If we know what could be the type of object, then it is far better to pass that as that type.

For some situations, though, using objects is mandatory, as in *event handlers*. Listing 3-14 finds methods in a given code that could have used a more specific type for some of its arguments than using an object.

Listing 3-14. Script to Find Object Obsessions

```
void Main()
{
        string code  =
        @"
        //Bad: "a" could have been more specifically typed.
        void fun(object a,int x,float d)
        {
        }
        void funny(int x)
        {
        }
        //Bad: This could have used more specific parameter type
        object soFunny(object one)
        {
            return one;
        }";

        var tree = CSharpSyntaxTree.ParseText(code);
        var result = tree.GetRoot()
                .DescendantNodes()
                .OfType<MethodDeclarationSyntax>()//#1
                .Where(thisMethod => //#2
                    //This method is not an event declaration
!thisMethod.IsEventDeclaration()
&& thisMethod.TakesOrReturnsObject())
                .Select(thisMethod =>
thisMethod.Identifier.ValueText); //#3
```

```
        if (result.Count() > 0)
        {
result.Dump(@"Methods that aren't event handlers but takes or
        returns objects");
        }
}

public static  class MethoDeclEx
{

        public static bool IsEventDeclaration
        (this MethodDeclarationSyntax mds)
        {
                return mds.ParameterList
                                    .Parameters
                                    .Any(p =>
                p.Type.ToFullString().EndsWith("EventArgs"));
        }

        public static bool TakesOrReturnsObject
        (this MethodDeclarationSyntax mds)
        {
                return mds.ParameterList
                        .Parameters
                        .Any(p =>

                        //If any parameter is of type object
                        p.Type.ToFullString().ToLower()
                                .Trim() == "object")

                        //if return type is of type object
                        || mds.ReturnType.ToFullString()
                        .ToLower().Trim() == "object";
        }
}
```

That code produces the output shown in Figure 3-16.

Methods that aren't event handlers but takes or returns objects

▲ IEnumerable<String> (2 items) ▶
fun
soFunny

Figure 3-16. *Methods that aren't event handlers but either take or return objects. These situations should be avoided.*

Extension methods declared in MethoDeclEx makes the code readable. Line #1 finds all the methods in the code. Line #2 filters out all other methods except the defaulter ones that take or return objects and aren't event handlers.

Summary

In this chapter you learned how Roslyn and LINQ can be used to extract several metrics to understand code health. In the next few chapters you will see how Roslyn can be used to detect plagiarism, generate dependency graphs, and identify design pattern usages.

CHAPTER 4

Code Performance Metrics

If you are programming for a while in an industrial setting, you know that most of the time, producing the right code that does what is expected is far more important than making sure it performs well. That said, in some systems performance considerations are of paramount importance. Getting your code to do the right thing *and fast* sometimes can be quite a challenge. Part of this challenge is to make sure that you know as a developer what will be the cost incurred in terms of running time for a coding construct. And because C#, like any other high-level language, lets you do the same thing in many ways, it becomes increasingly hard to keep abreast of the performance penalties due for coding constructs as newer versions of frameworks become available.

In this chapter you'll see how Roslyn can be used to find out costly constructs. Some of these are conventional wisdom. But till now, we as developers had to wait till an assembly got generated to test the constraints. Roslyn changed that.

Each section starts with a header explaining the problem originating from a particular coding construct and then includes a script to find code that uses that construct. Finally, an explanation of the script is provided.

The heading for each section lists a common piece of wisdom in .NET. These are nothing new, so little explanation is provided for the rationale on why this piece of advice makes sense to make the code more performant. On the other hand, detailed explanation is provided on the script (Roslyn/LINQ) that finds segments of code that fail to adhere to the guideline named in the heading of each section.

Avoid Boxing

Boxing and unboxing are costly operations because they copy and then dereference an object to the desited type. Please avoid using these as most as you can. Listing 4-1 shows how to find them.

Listing 4-1. Script to Find Boxing/Unboxing Calls

```
var code =
@"public void fun()
        {
                int x = 32;
                Point p = new Point(10, 10);
                object box = p;
                p.x = 20;
                Console.Write(((Point)box).x);
                object o = x;
        }";
```

© Sudipta Mukherjee 2016
S. Mukherjee, *Source Code Analytics With Roslyn and JavaScript Data Visualization*,
DOI 10.1007/978-1-4842-1925-6_4

```
var tree = CSharpSyntaxTree.ParseText(code);//#1

//There are couple of boxing calls in the provided code sample
//These should have been avoided
//x - Int
//o -> object

var objects =

tree.GetRoot()
    .DescendantNodes()    .OfType<VariableDeclarationSyntax>()//#2
.SelectMany(aes => aes.Variables.Select(v =>
        new //#3
            {
                Type = aes.GetFirstToken().ValueText,
               Name = v.Identifier.ValueText,
               Value = aes.GetLastToken().ValueText
            })
);
var defaulters = objects //#4
              .Where(aes => aes.Type == "object"
          && objects.FirstOrDefault(d => d.Name == aes.Value
          && d.Type!="object") != null )

.Dump("Boxing calls");
```

The preceding code produces the output shown in Figure 4-1.

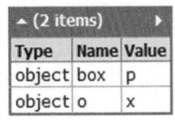

Figure 4-1. *Defaulters for boxing calls*

In the code, the line marked #1 creates the source tree from the code given. Then line #2 finds all the variable declaration statements. Line #3 creates a projection of these variable declarations with three pieces of metadata, namely Type, Name (of the variable), and Value (the actual value of the object). Then line #4 filters out everything, leaving only the ones that will result in a boxing call in the IL.

Avoid Using dynamic by Default

The dynamic keyword was invented for interacting with dynamic programming languages from statically typed programming languages like C#. Although the compiler won't complain when you use it in places where it is not needed, as in Listing 4-2, refrain from it because it causes a performance penalty.

Listing 4-2. Script to Find All dynamic Variables

```
var code =
@"static void Main(string[] args)
{
  dynamic a = 13;
  dynamic b = 14;
  dynamic c = a + b;
  Console.WriteLine(c);
}";

var tree = CSharpSyntaxTree.ParseText(code);//#1

tree.GetRoot()
    .DescendantNodes()
    .OfType<VariableDeclarationSyntax>()//#2
    //#3
    .Where(vds => vds.Type.ToFullString().Trim() == "dynamic")
    .Select(vds => vds.ToFullString())
    .Dump("All usages of dynamic. Some may not be required");
```

The preceding code produces the output shown in Figure 4-2.

All usages of dynamic. Some may not be required

▲ IEnumerable<String> (3 items) ▶
dynamic a = 13
dynamic b = 14
dynamic c = a + b

Figure 4-2. *All dynamic variables*

Line #1 creates the syntax tree from the given source code. Line #2 finds all the variable declarations, and line #3 filters everything out except the dynamic ones. One thing to notice, though, is that I have not mapped these declarations with any class or method declaration. But I had developed several examples in the book to give you an idea about how to do that. Try to change the script to find all the dynamic variable declarations per class. That will really give you an idea about how to change these scripts to find defaulters across multiple labels of modularity in your codebase.

Avoid Excessive Local Variables

The recommendation is to use fewer than 64 variables per function, but for demonstration purposes I have chosen to only 4 variables. You can imagine how troublesome it would be to wrap your head around 64 variables and their purposes! Listing 4-3 shows how to find methods with many variables.

Listing 4-3. Script to Find Methods with Lot of Local Variables

```
var code = @"void fun()
{
        int x;
        int y;
        int z;
        int w;
        int ws;
 }";

var tree = CSharpSyntaxTree.ParseText(code);//#1

//The recommended value is 64;
//But for deomonstration purpose it is changed to 4
const int MAX_LOCALS_ALLOWED = 4; //#2

tree.GetRoot()
    .DescendantNodes()
        .OfType<MethodDeclarationSyntax>() //#3
        .Where(mds =>
         mds.Body.Statements
            .OfType<LocalDeclarationStatementSyntax>()
            .Count()>=MAX_LOCALS_ALLOWED) //#4
        .Select(mds => mds.Identifier.ValueText)//#5
        .Dump("Methods with many local variable declarations");
```

The preceding code produces the output shown in Figure 4-3.

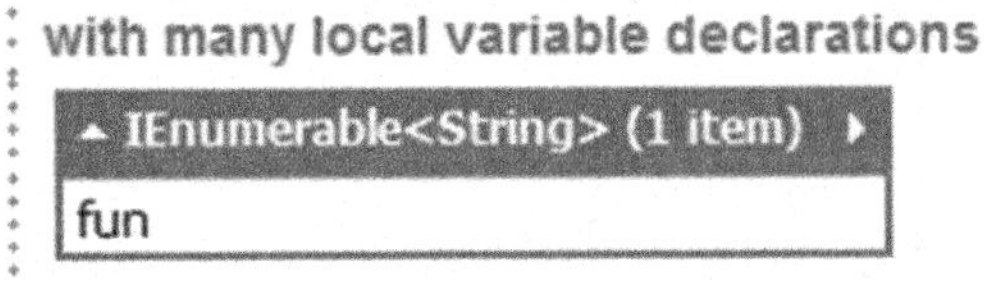

Figure 4-3. *Methods with lots of local variables*

Line #1 parses the given source code to generate the syntax tree. Line #2 marks the constant for the maximum number of local variables to be allowed. The MSDN guideline says this number should be 64, but for demonstration purposes I have set this constant to 4. Even though 64 is recommended by Microsoft, I strongly feel that anything beyond 10 local variables is a sign of a bad design choice and poses a serious hindrance for maintenance. Line #3 finds all the local variable declarations. The filtering clause at line #4 filters out everything else except the methods that have more than four local variables declared. Finally, the projection at line #5 projects the names of those defaulter methods.

This script finds methods with lots of local variables. Try to modify it so that it finds variable declarations at the class level.

Prefer Literals Over Evaluation

I was debugging some code, and one particular construct caught my attention, and I couldn't resist laughing. I think that this is hilarious and is a case that should be avoided at all costs. This type of mistake can become really costly if these calls are within a loop or such repetitive calls.

The question you may be pondering is how such constructs can creep into the codebase. Well, the probable reason might be that GetEdgeRepr() used to return "EDGE", and at one point it started returning "edge". So, to cater to this change in the behavior of GetEdgeRepr(), a ToLower() call is shoved at the end—that way it will be easier to get back to "EDGE" if GetEdgeRepr() starts to return "EDGE" again. But that's a really bad argument, and the resulting code is ugly and inefficient. A better approach would have been to shove the ToLower() at the end of GetEdgeRepr(). But ideally we should minimize the number of calls to ToLower() and ToUpper() if we know what exactly will be outcome, as shown in Figure 4-4.

```
string edgeRepr = GetEdgeRepr();
if ("EDGE".ToLower() == edgeRepr)
{
    //Do Something.
}
```

Figure 4-4. *Code that uses* ToLower() *on literal. Such calls should be avoided.*

What's the problem with the preceding code snippet? Every time this code is called, "EDGE" will be transformed to "edge" and checked against the value returned by the GetEdgeRepr function. Instead, it should have been written like this:

```
if ("edge" == edgeRepr)
{
  // Do Something
}
```

Listing 4-4 finds such occurrences of source code.

Listing 4-4. Script to Find Bad Unnecessary Usage of ToUpper, ToLower, and So Forth on Strings

```
//Avoid using ToLower(), ToUpper() on string literals
var code =
@"class A
{
        public string fun()
        {
          int x = ""EDGE"".Length;
          string s  = ""Edge"".Substring(1,4);
          return ""EDGE"".ToLower();
          ""234"".TryParse();
        }
```

```
        public string GetRep(string upper)
        {
            return upper.ToLower();
        }
}";

var tree = CSharpSyntaxTree.ParseText(code); //#1

    //Finding all the literals in the code.
    var literals = tree.GetRoot()
                        .DescendantNodes()
                        .OfType<LiteralExpressionSyntax>()//#2
                        .Select(les => les.ToFullString())
                        .Distinct();

tree.GetRoot()
    .DescendantNodes()
    .OfType<InvocationExpressionSyntax>()
    .Select(ies => new    //#3
        {
                MethodName = ies.Ancestors()
                .OfType<MethodDeclarationSyntax>()
                ?.First()?.Identifier.ValueText,
                Expression = ies.Expression.ToFullString(),
                CallTokens = ies.Expression.ChildNodes()
                            .Select(e => e.ToFullString())
        })
//#4
.Where(ies => ies.CallTokens.Any(ct => literals.Contains(ct)))
//#5
.Select(ies =>
            new
                {
                        MethodName = ies.MethodName,
                        Expression = ies.Expression
                })

.Dump("Methods using ToUpper or ToLower on string literals");
```

The preceding code produces the output shown in Figure 4-5.

Methods using ToUpper or ToLower on string literals

▲ (3 items)   ▶

MethodName	Expression
fun	"Edge".Substring
fun	"EDGE".ToLower
fun	"234".TryParse

Figure 4-5. *Methods that use ToUpper() or ToLower() on string literals, which should have been avoided*

Line #1 parses the source code to create the syntax tree. Line #2 finds all the literal expressions in the source code. Line #3 creates a projection for all method invocations along with names of the method, call tokens, and the expression of invocation. This information will be helpful in locating the methods that call string methods on string literals.

The filtering clause at line #4 filters out everything else apart from the methods for which call tokens have a trace of a string literal, seen before in the code. This could be an indication that the method is actually called on the string literal, or it may not.

Line #5 creates a projection of the method name and the expression that uses a string literal in the call. This is the defaulter list for this rule.

Avoid volatile Declarations

Limit the use of the volatile keyword because volatile fields restrict the way the compiler reads and writes the contents of the field. The compiler generates the code that always reads from the field's memory location instead of reading from a register that may have loaded the field's value. This means that accessing volatile fields is slower than nonvolatile ones because the system is forced to use memory addresses rather than registers.

Thus, using volatile is not good for performance reasons. Don't use it unless absolutely required. Listing 4-5 shows how to find usages of volatile in a given codebase.

Listing 4-5. Script to Find Usages of volatile in C# Code

```
var code =
@"class VolatileTest
{
    public volatile int i;

    public void Test(int _i)
    {
        i = _i;
    }
}";

var tree = CSharpSyntaxTree.ParseText(code);//#1

tree.GetRoot()
        .DescendantNodes()
        .OfType<FieldDeclarationSyntax>()//#2
        .Where(vds => vds.Modifiers
                    .Any(m => m.ValueText == "volatile"))//#3
        .Select(vds => new //#4
        {
                ClassName = vds.Ancestors()
                    .OfType<ClassDeclarationSyntax>()
                    .First()?.Identifier.ValueText,
                VolatileDeclaration = vds.ToFullString()
        })
        .Dump();
```

That code produces the output shown in Figure 4-6.

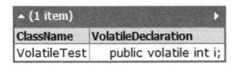

Figure 4-6. *Types with volatile fields*

Line #1 creates the source syntax tree from the given source code. Line #2 finds all the variable declarations in the class. The Where clause at line #3 finds all fields marked with a volatile modifier. Finally, at line #4, this data gets projected for classes and their volatile declarations.

Don't Use an Object Array in params

The params array should be strongly typed because otherwise the receiving function or the called function that takes these parameters will have to cast them back to something before using, and that causes a performance penalty. Thus it is advisable not to use an object array in params. Listing 4-6 helps find blocks of code that fail to satisfy this rule.

Listing 4-6. Script to Find Code that Uses Object Arrays in params

```
string code =
@"class A
 {
  bool someSearchWithObjParams(params object[] searchTerms)
  {
  }
  bool someSearch(params objectsome [] searchCriteria)
  {
        //Do some search
  }
  bool search(int a,int b, params string[] arra)
  {
  }
  bool search(string code, int length)
  {
  }
}";

var tree = CSharpSyntaxTree.ParseText(code);//#1

tree.GetRoot()
    .DescendantNodes()
        .OfType<MethodDeclarationSyntax>()//#2
        .Where(mds => mds.ParameterList.Parameters
                .Any(p => p.Modifiers
                        .Any(m => m.Text == "params" && //#3
                p.Type.ToFullString().Replace(" ",string.Empty)
.Contains("object[]"))))
```

```
.Select(mds => new //#4
{
        //Name of the class
        ClassName = mds.Ancestors()
                        .OfType<ClassDeclarationSyntax>()
                        .First()
                                    .Identifier
                                    .ValueText,
        //The name of defaulter method
        MethodName = mds.Identifier.ValueText
})
.Dump("Methods with param objects");
```

The preceding code produces the output shown in Figure 4-7.

Figure 4-7. *Class and methods with object param array*

Line #1 creates the source syntax tree from the given source code. Line #2 finds all the method declarations from the given code. Line #3 finds those methods that take a loosely typed param array (that is, object array as params). Line #4 creates a projection with class names and defaulter method names.

Avoid Unnecessary Projections

Deferred execution means that unless absolutely required, LINQ queries don't get executed to generate the result set. It is lazy that way. If you have got an IEnumerable<T> from a method as a returned type, it is enough to be able to iterate over that because foreach can iterate over anything that is enumerable. Therefore, it is not required to project that as a strongly typed list using ToList or to a strongly typed array using ToArray, and so on. These calls are expensive because they create a new list and run through the enumerable to retrieve each element from it and add to the newly created list. Therefore, having this unnecessary projection means that on the consumer side, the program will have to run through twice the length of the enumerable. So it is advisable not to use projections for variable declarations.

The main motivation for this is visual studio degbugging facility. Before VS 2015, enumerating an IEnumerable<T> in QuickWatch wasn't possible. This kind of forced developers to shove in a .ToList() or a .ToArray() at the end of the variable declaration, so that they could view the values inside the collection using common visual studio debugging tools like QuickWatch, Add Watch, and so on. However on some occassions, developers forget to unplug these extra calls before building for release mode. Listing 4-7 shows how to find unnecessary projections.

Listing 4-7. Script to Find Unnecessary Projections

```
var code = @"class A
            {
                    void fun(IEnumerable<int> nums)
                    {
                        var vals = nums.ToList();
                    foreach(var v in vals)
                    {
                        ...
                    }
                }
            }";
var tree = CSharpSyntaxTree.ParseText(code);//#1

var decls = tree
        .GetRoot()
        .DescendantNodes()
        .OfType<LocalDeclarationStatementSyntax>();//#2

var projectors = new string[]{".ToList();",".ToArray();"};
if (decls.Count() > 0) //#3
{
        var defaulters = decls.Select(ldss => new //#4
        {
                ClassName = ldss.Ancestors()
                            .OfType<ClassDeclarationSyntax>()
                            .FirstOrDefault()
                            ?.Identifier
                            .ValueText,
                Method = ldss.Ancestors()
                            .OfType<MethodDeclarationSyntax>()
                            .FirstOrDefault()?.Identifier
                            .ValueText,
                Statement = ldss.ToFullString().Trim()
    })
    //#5
    .Where(ldss => projectors
        .Any(projector => ldss.Statement.Trim()
          .EndsWith(projector)));

    if(defaulters.Count() > 0)
      defaulters.Dump("Un-necessary projections");
}
```

The preceding code produces the output shown in Figure 4-8.

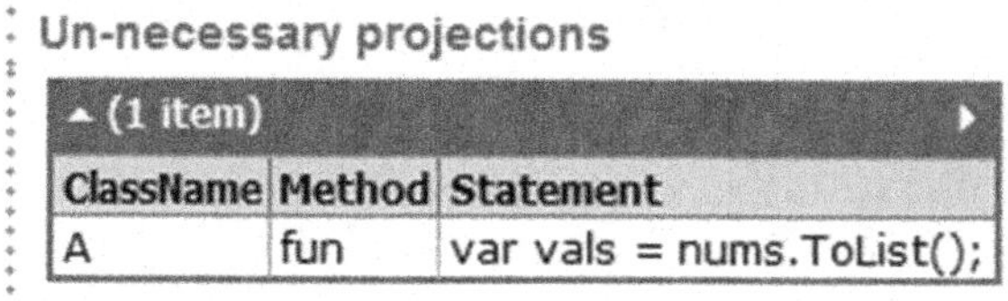

Un-necessary projections

(1 item)

ClassName	Method	Statement
A	fun	var vals = nums.ToList();

Figure 4-8. *Classes with unnecessary projections*

Line #1 creates the syntax tree from the source code. Line #2 finds all the local variable declarations in the given source code. Line #3 checks whether there is at least one such instance of local variable declaration or not. Line #4 creates a projection with the name of the class where this method that holds the local variable declaration belongs, the name of the method and the local variable declaration statement itself.

Line #5 filters out everything except those variable declarations that end with a projector (either has a `ToList` or a `ToArray` at the end of the variable declaration statement).

I urge you to measure the performance gain/penalty from not using/using these projectors at the variable declarations. You'll see that dropping these makes the program run about 10 percent faster.

Value Types Should Override Equals and GetHashCode

From MSDN, this rule is also known as CA1815. The description goes like this:

For value types, the inherited implementation of `Equals` uses the Reflection library and compares the contents of all fields. Reflection is computationally expensive, and comparing every field for equality might be unnecessary. If you expect users to compare or sort instances, or use them as hash table keys, your value type should implement `Equals`. If your programming language supports operator overloading, you should also provide an implementation of the equality and inequality operators.

Listing 4-8 finds such code issues.

Listing 4-8. Script to Find Structs without Either `Equals` or `GetHashCode` Not Overridden

```
//structs types must provide overrides for Equals() and GetHashCode()

var code = @"struct Vector : IEquatable<Vector>
{
  public int X { get; set; }
  public int Y { get; set; }
  public int Z { get; set; }

  public int Magnitude { get; set; }

  public override bool Equals(object obj)
  {
    if (obj == null)
    {
      return false;
    }
```

```
  if (obj.GetType() != this.GetType())
  {
    return false;
  }
  return this.Equals((Vector)obj);
}

public bool Equals(Vector other)
{
  return this.X == other.X
    && this.Y == other.Y
    && this.Z == other.Z
    && this.Magnitude == other.Magnitude;
}

 //Deliberately commented to make this struct a "defaulter"
 //public override int GetHashCode()
 //{
 //   return X ^ Y ^ Z ^ Magnitude;
 //}
}";

var tree = CSharpSyntaxTree.ParseText(code);//#1

tree.GetRoot()
    .DescendantNodes()
        .OfType<StructDeclarationSyntax>()//#2
        .Select(sds => new  //#3
        {
                StructName = sds.Identifier.ValueText,
            //Flag if "Equals" is overridden
              OverridenEquals =
              sds.Members
                   .OfType<MethodDeclarationSyntax>()
                   .FirstOrDefault(m => m.Identifier
               .ValueText == "Equals"
                 && m.Modifiers.Any(mo =>
                mo.ValueText == "override")) != null,
            //Flag if "GetHashCode" is overridden
              OverridenGetHashCode =
              sds.Members
                 .OfType<MethodDeclarationSyntax>()
                   .FirstOrDefault(m => m.Identifier
              .ValueText == "GetHashCode"
                && m.Modifiers.Any(mo =>
               mo.ValueText == "override"))!=null
        })
        .Where(sds => !sds.OverridenEquals
                  || !sds.OverridenGetHashCode)//#4
        .Dump("Defaulter Structs");
```

This code produces the output shown in Figure 4-9.

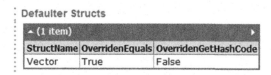

Figure 4-9. *Structs that don't override either the* `Equals` *or* `GetHashCode` *methods*

Line #1 parses the source code and creates the syntax tree. Line #2 finds all the struct declarations in the given source code sample. Line #3 creates a projection with the name of the struct and couple of flags indicating whether the methods `Equals` and `GetHashCode` have been overridden or not. Line #4 filters out every other struct declaration except the defaulter ones that don't have both of these methods overridden.

Avoid Using Empty Strings to Find Zero Length Strings

This is a rule from Microsoft Peformance warning. Here is the description from MSDN :

Comparing strings using the `String.Length` property or the `String.IsNullOrEmpty` method is significantly faster than using `Equals`. This is because `Equals` executes significantly more MSIL instructions than either `IsNullOrEmpty` or the number of instructions executed to retrieve the `Length` property value and compare it to zero.

You should be aware that `Equals` and `Length == 0` behave differently for null strings. If you try to get the value of the `Length` property on a null string, the *common language runtime* (CLR) throws a `System.NullReferenceException`. If you perform a comparison between a null string and the empty string, the CLT does not throw an exception; the comparison returns `false`. Testing for null does not significantly affect the relative performance of these two approaches. When targeting .NET Framework 2.0, use the `IsNullOrEmpty` method. Otherwise, use the `Length == comparison` whenever possible.

Listing 4-9 finds such bad uses.

Listing 4-9. Script to Find Cases Where Empty Strings Are Used to Check Length of String

```
string code =
@"using System;
namespace PerformanceLibrary
{
        public class StringTester
        {
                string s1 = ""test"";
                public void EqualsTest()
                {
                        if (s1 == """")
                        {
                                Console.WriteLine(@""s1 equals empty
                                string."");
                        }
                }
```

```csharp
            public void LengthTest()
            {
                if (s1 != null && s1.Length == 0)
                {
                    Console.WriteLine(""s1.Length == 0."");
                }
            }

            public void NullOrEmptyTest()
            {
                if (!String.IsNullOrEmpty(s1))
                {
                    Console.WriteLine(""s1 != null and
                     s1.Length != 0."");
                }
            }
        }
}";
var tree = CSharpSyntaxTree.ParseText(code);//#1
//Finding all instances of "string" in source code.
var strings = tree
            .GetRoot()
            .DescendantNodes()
            .OfType<VariableDeclarationSyntax>()//#2
            .Where(vds => vds.Type.ToFullString().Trim() ==
                "string")//#3
            .SelectMany(vds => vds.Variables.Select(v =>
                    v.Identifier.ValueText));//#4

    var results  = tree.GetRoot()
            .DescendantNodes()
            .OfType<IfStatementSyntax>()
            .Where(iss => strings
    .Any(s => iss.Condition.ToFullString()
        .Contains(s + " == \"\""))) //#5
            .Select(iss => new //#6
            {
                MethodName = iss.Ancestors()
                    .OfType<MethodDeclarationSyntax>()
                    .First()
                    .Identifier.ValueText,
                Condition = iss.ToFullString()
            });

            if(results.Any())
                    results.Dump();
```

Thpreceding code produces the output shown in Figure 4-10.

▲ (1 item)	▶
MethodName	**Condition**

EqualsTest	if (s1 == "")
	     {
	        Console.WriteLine("s1 equals empty string.");
	     }

Figure 4-10. *Defaulter method that uses empty string to find zero length strings*

Line #1 creates the syntax tree from the source code. Line #2 finds all the variable declarations. Line #3 finds all of the variables that are of type string. Line #4 projects the names of these string variables.

The filtering clause at line #5 filters out everything except the ones that use one string variable in a string comparison with an empty string. The projection at line #6 helps create a defaulter list consisting of the names of the methods and the conditional statements that fail this test.

Prefer "Jagged" Arrays over Multidimentional Arrays

A *jagged* array is an array whose elements are arrays. The arrays that make up the elements can be of different sizes, leading to less wasted space for some sets of data.

Listing 4-10 finds all those classes that have multidimentional arrays.

Listing 4-10. Script to Find Types with Multidimensional Arrays

```
string code = @"using System;
namespace PerformanceLibrary
{
    public class ArrayHolder
    {
        int[][] jaggedArray = { new int[] {1,2,3,4},
                                new int[] {5,6,7},
                                new int[] {8},
                                new int[] {9}
                              };

        int [ , ] multiDimArray = {{1,2,3,4},
                                   {5,6,7,0},
                                   {8,0,0,0},
                                   {9,0,0,0}
                                  };
    }
}
";
```

```
var tree = CSharpSyntaxTree.ParseText(code);//#1

tree.GetRoot()
    .DescendantNodes()
        .OfType<ArrayRankSpecifierSyntax>()//#2
        .Select(ats => new //#3
        {
                BelongsTo = ats.Ancestors()
.OfType<ClassDeclarationSyntax>()
            .First()?.Identifier.ValueText,
                ArrayType = ats.ToFullString()
        })
        .Where(ats => ats.ArrayType.Contains(","))//#4
        .Dump("Classes with multi-dimentional array");
```

That code produces the output shown in Figure 4-11.

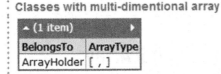

Figure 4-11. *Classes with multidimentional arrays*

Line #1 creates the syntax tree from source code. Line #2 finds all multiple dimentional arrays (either jagged or regular *multi-dim*) declarations. Line #3 projects the name of the class where this array is being declared and the type of the array. The filtering clause at line #4 finds those types (classes) with multidimentional array in them.

Don't Return Array from a Property

Arrays returned by properties are not write-protected, even if the property is read-only. To keep the array tamper-proof, the property must return a copy of the array. Typically, users will not understand the adverse performance implications of calling such a property. Specifically, they might use the property as an indexed property.

Listing 4-11 finds such properties.

Listing 4-11. Script to Find Properties Returning Arrays

```
string code =

@"using System;
namespace PerformanceLibrary
{
    public class Test
    {
        string [] nameValues;
        public Test()
        {
```

```
            nameValues = new string[100];
            for (int i = 0; i< 100; i++)
            {
                nameValues[i] = ""Sample"";
            }
        }
        public string[] Names
        {
                get
                {
                        return (string[])nameValues.Clone();
                }
        }
    public static void Main()
    {
        // Using the property in the following manner
        // results in 201 copies of the array.
        // One copy is made each time the loop executes,
        // and one copy is made each time the condition is
        // tested.

        Test t = new Test();

        for (int i = 0; i < t.Names.Length; i++)
        {
                if (t.Names[i] == (""SomeName""))
                {
                        // Perform some operation.
                }
        }
    }
    }
    }
}
";
var tree = CSharpSyntaxTree.ParseText(code);//#1
tree.GetRoot()
        .DescendantNodes()
        .OfType<ClassDeclarationSyntax>()//#2
        .Select(cds => new //#3
        {
                ClassName = cds.Identifier.ValueText,
                Properties = cds.Members
                .OfType<PropertyDeclarationSyntax>()
                  .Select(pds => new //#4
                  {
                        PropertyName = pds.Identifier.ValueText,
                        PropertyType = pds.Type.ToFullString()
                                            .Trim()
                })
        })
```

```
    .Where(cds => cds.Properties //#5
        .Any(p => p.PropertyType.Contains("[")))

    .Dump("Properties returning an array");
```

The preceding code produces the output shown in Figure 4-12.

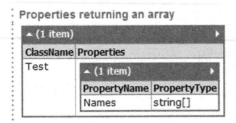

Figure 4-12. *Properties that return arrays*

Line #1 creates the syntax tree from the source code. Line #2 finds all the class declarations in the given source code. Line #3 creates a projection with all the names of the classes along with the names and types of the properties they host. Line #4 creates the inner projection for each property of each class. Line #5 filters out everything else except the ones returning arrays.

Don't Use Thread.Abort or Thread.Suspend

Avoid using Thread.Abort to terminate other threads. When you call Abort, the CLR throws a ThreadAbortException. Calling Abort does not immediately result in thread termination. It causes an exception on the thread to be terminated. You can use Thread.Join to wait on the thread to make sure that the thread has terminated.

Never call Thread.Suspend and Thread.Resume to synchronize the activities of multiple threads. Do not call Suspend to suspend low priority threads—consider setting the Thread.Priority property instead of controlling the threads intrusively.

Calling Suspend on one thread from the other is a highly intrusive process that can result in serious application deadlocks. For example, you might suspend a thread that is holding onto resources needed by other threads or the thread that called Suspend.

Listing 4-12 finds such uses as Thread.Abort and Thread.Suspend.

Listing 4-12. Script to Find Thread.Abort and Thread.Suspend Calls

```
string code =
@" public static void Main()
{
        Thread newThread   =
            new Thread(new ThreadStart(TestMethod));
        newThread.Start();
        Thread.Sleep(1000);

        // Abort newThread.
        Console.WriteLine(""Main aborting new thread."");
```

```
        newThread.Abort(""Information from Main."");

        // Wait for the thread to terminate.
         newThread.Join();
         Console.WriteLine(@""New thread terminated -
                             Main exiting."");
}";

var tree = CSharpSyntaxTree.ParseText(code);//#1

//Finding names of all "Thread" objects
var allThreadNames =
     tree.GetRoot()
         .DescendantNodes()
         .OfType<LocalDeclarationStatementSyntax>()//#2
         .Where(ldss => ldss.Declaration.Type
         .ToFullString().Trim() == "Thread" ||
         ldss.Declaration.Type.ToFullString().Trim()
                 == "System.Threading.Thread")//#3
         .SelectMany(ldss => ldss.Declaration.Variables
           .Select(v => v.Identifier.ValueText));//#4

//Finding all the method invocations
tree.GetRoot()
       .DescendantNodes()
       .OfType<InvocationExpressionSyntax>()//#5
       .Where(ies => allThreadNames
            .Any(tn =>  ies.Expression.ToFullString()
              .Trim().StartsWith(tn+".Abort")//#6
|| ies.Expression.ToFullString()
                   .Trim().StartsWith(tn + ".Suspend")))
       .Select(d => new //#7
       {
               Method = d.Ancestors()
                     .OfType<MethodDeclarationSyntax>()
                     .First().Identifier.ValueText,
               Line = d.Expression.ToFullString().Trim()
       })
       .Dump("Defaulters");
```

The preceding code produces the output shown in Figure 4-13.

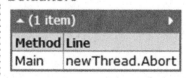

Figure 4-13. *Methods using Thread.Abort or Thread.Suspend*

Line #1 parses the source code to create the syntax tree. Line #2 finds all the local variable declarations. Line #3 finds all Thread variables declared, and line #4 projects their names such that later calls of Abort or Suspend can be identified on these named objects.

Line #5 finds all the method invocations (or method calls) in the source code. Line #6 finds all those calls to either Thread.Abort or Thread.Suspend for any of the identified thread objects.

Line #7 creates a projection of the defaulter list with the method names and the line in the method that calls to Thread.Abort or Thread.Suspend.

As you can see, you can easily extend this script to support other thread methods like Thread.Resume.

Summary

In this chapter you learned how to use Roslyn and plain C# to find gotchas in your C# code that could cause some performance penalty. Some of these rules are taken from https://msdn.microsoft.com/en-us/library/ff647790.aspx and some from https://msdn.microsoft.com/en-US/library/ms182260.aspx.

This chapter presents a decent catalogue of coding constructs to be wary of for performance penalties. I hope you got the idea of how to code to find the specific one you might be interested in digging for in your codebase.

In the next chapter you'll see how Roslyn can be used to mine code to extract several useful patterns from source code. See you there!

CHAPTER 5

Code Mining

Code is art, and like other art forms like music and painting, good source code exhibits similar patterns. These are not only design patterns—they are regular code patterns that occur frequently. The information about code patterns can be helpful in a multitude of situations.

Useful Patterns in Code Mining

For example, these patterns can be useful in identifying *duplicate to near duplicate* code blocks, checking the difference between two versions of the same code, identifying dependancies, detecting plagiarism, and understanding the construction of the code better by *knowledge mining*.

Identifying Near Duplicate Code

Near duplicate code means two or more instances of code that are same or almost same are same semantically. Sometimes developers work on a tight deadline. That means less time for refactoring. Also in a huge codebase, it's not hard to find logically duplicate or almost duplicate methods in codebases. Identifying such similar methods and giving them much-needed refactoring reduces *technical debt*.

Take a look at these two samples shown in Figure 5-1. These represent a classic duplicate code situation. Only the boxed parts have been changed. Agreed with LINQ, people might just use Average(), but this code is for demonstration purpose.

```
public double calcAvgSal(List<double> salaries)
{
    double sum = 0;

    for(int i = 0; i<salaries.Count ; i++)
        sum += salaries[i];

    return sum/salaries.Count;
}
```

```
public double calcAvgBonus(List<double> bonuses)
{
    double sum = 0;

    for(int i = 0; i<bonuses.Count ; i++)
        sum += bonuses[i];

    return sum/bonuses.Count;
}
```

Figure 5-1. *Near duplicate code side by side*

S. Mukherjee, *Source Code Analytics With Roslyn and JavaScript Data Visualization*,
DOI 10.1007/978-1-4842-1925-6_5

That example is obvious, but consider a subtler code duplication situation. Look at the two samples shown in Figure 5-2.

```
void fun()                          void fun()
{                                   {
        int x = 0;                          int y = 0;
        if(x<1)                             doThose(y);
         dothat();                  }
        else                        void doThose(int y)
         doThis();                  {
}                                           if(y <1)
                                                dothat();
                                            else
                                                doThis();
                                   }
```

Figure 5-2. *Subtle example of plagiarism*

If these two blocks were compared in a line-by-line comparer like Beyond Compare, the comparer won't catch that these two functions are exactly the same. Although the line-by-line comparer had some success in identifying that the code samples in the previous examples are similar, the comparer will fail to distinguish between these two effectively.

Plagarism Detection

Students copy from each other or get source code from publicly available sources online and then play smart by just changing variable names, method names, class names, and so on before submitting their code. A naïve checker fails to recognize semantically identical codes. Consider the following couple of methods extracted from code submissions for a project from two students namely Mark and Tony, as shown in Figure 5-3. (These are fictitious names—no connections to anyone whatsoever.)

```
Mark's submission               Tony's submission

int fun(int x)                  int update(int number)
{                               {
  for(int j = 0;j<10;j++)          for(int loopCounter = 0;loopCounter<10;loopCounter++)
      x++;                             number++;
  return x++;                     return number+1;
}                               }
```

Figure 5-3. *Two fictitious example submissions*

When compared with Beyond Compare, I got the result shown in Figure 5-4.

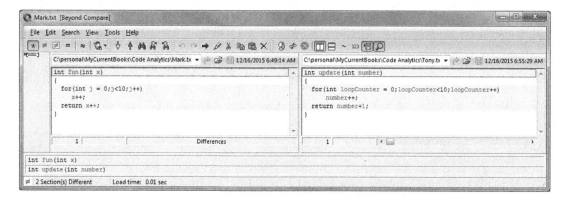

Figure 5-4. *Please write caption here*

Although Beyond Compare correctly identifies what is changed, being a line-by-line checker, it does what it is supposed to do. However, these methods are structurally the same and do the exact same things. In other words, these methods are semantically the same. Beyond Compare fails to identify that.

Source Code Forensics

Imagine that two students submit code and it looks plagiarized. Should the credit be given to one of them for originality? If so, which one? Who might be the original author, and who might have been plagiarizing? The only way to know is to look at submissions historically. The credit for originality should be given to the student whose code remained similar in patterns, historically. This technique is known as *code forensics* or *source code forensics*. Using Roslyn and a little machine learning (ML) technique, the original author can be identified. Later in the book, you'll see how this can be done on fake submissions.

Knowledge Mining

When a new team member comes aboard, she might find it challenging to understand rationals behind design choices in a huge codebase. Roslyn APIs (Syntax and Semantic Analysis APIs) can be used to determine the structures in the source code that can help new members see the so-called *big picture* from the source code.

In this chapter, you'll see how Roslyn and LINQ-to-Objects can be used to perform some of those operations.

SmartDiff: A Smart Code Comparer

Consider the code blocks shown side by side in Figure 5-5. These are fabricated toy examples, so please don't focus on the meaning of method or class definitions. Rather, I urge you to look at the function signatures and the implementation.

```
class A                              class B
{                                    {
    public void fun(int a)
    {                                    public int m2()
        a++;                             {
    }                                        return 23;
}                                        }
class B                                  //public int m1()//old
{                                    //   {
    public int m1()                  //       return 22;
    {                                //   }
        return 2;                        public int m1()
    }                                    {
    public int m2()                          return 2;
    {                                    }
        return 23;                   }
    }                                class A
}                                    {
                                         public void fun(int a)
                                         {
                                             a++;
                                         }
                                     }
```

Figure 5-5. *Two semantically same code blocks side-by-side*

If you pause for a while you'll see that they are identical semantically. But these types of semantically similar code blocks can't be found using line-by-line comparers like Beyond Compare.

In this section, you'll see how to use the Roslyn Syntax API to build a smart *diff* tool. The objective of this tool is to generate humane outputs like the following, that describe the changes:

```
The parameter "age" is dropped from the method "UpdateProfile" in class "AgeManager" in
version 2

The method "Update" is not found in class "AgeManager" in version 1
```

Anatomy of a Code Block

Before we go deep into implementing the smart comparer, let's see what the different parts of the code blocks are that we want to compare—like properties, methods, and so on.

Anatomy of a Property Declaration

A property can have all or some of these parts in its declaration:

```
Attributes
Modifiers
Property Name
Property Type
Body for the getter
Body for the setter
```

Figure 5-6 shows a sample property declaration with all these parts.

```
[Obsolete]
[Deprecated]
public static int AgeOld
{
  get
  {
      if (age < 0)
          return age + 10;
  }
  set
  {
      age = value;
  }
}
```

Figure 5-6. *Sample property with several parts*

[Obsolete] and [Depricated] are the attributes of the property AgeOld and the modifiers are public and static. As you can see, the property is called AgeOld and it is of type int. Each property is defined within a class. So, while comparing properties from multiple classes in multiple versions, we will have to take that into account. Besides these parts, a property like any other code segment can have a leading and a trailing trivia. Properties can also have leading structured trivia (which is nothing but the XML comment).

Anatomy of a Method

As you can see, the parts of a method are as follows:

```
Attributes
Modifiers
Method Name
Return Type
Constraint Clauses
Parameter types
Body
```

Figure 5-7 shows an example of these parts in a method declaration.

```
/// <summary>
///
/// </summary>
/// <param name=""tran""></param>
/// <param name=""dt""></param>
/// <param name=""updateMaster""></param>
/// <returns></returns>
[STAThread]
[MandatoryOperation]
public BankAccount UpdateDetails<T>(Transaction<T> tran, DateTime dt, bool updateMaster)
                    where T : class
{
    //Body
    //...
    //..
}
```

Figure 5-7. *Parts of a method*

[STAThread] and [MandatoryOperation] are attributes. The method UpdateDetails<T> is public. So the access modifer or the modifiers are public. The method works only if the parameter is a class. Thus the constraint clause is "where T: class". There are three parameters of the method with types as Transaction<T>, DateTime, and bool respectively. The method returns a new BankAccount object, presuming that there exists a class called BankAccount.

Listing 5-1 shows how to build a smart comparer of C# code that ignores the order in the declaration and checks a couple of code blocks. All the pieces of this system are made available as GitHub gists, because it would be incredibly hard to follow along otherwise.

Listing 5-1. A Very Basic but Smart Code Comparer for C#

```
//Written using Microsoft.CodeAnalysis.CSharp and LINQ
public class SmartComparer
{
    public static string Code1 { get; set; } //#1
    public static string Code2 { get; set; } //#2

    public static IEnumerable<ClassDeclarationSyntax>
                Classes1 { get; set; } //#3
    public static IEnumerable<ClassDeclarationSyntax>
                Classes2 { get; set; }//#4
    public static SyntaxTree Tree1 //#5
    {
        get
        {
            return CSharpSyntaxTree.ParseText(Code1);
        }
    }
    public static SyntaxTree Tree2 //#6
    {
        get
        {
            return CSharpSyntaxTree.ParseText(Code2);
        }
    }
```

```
    public static string MethodCompareMessage //#7
    {
           get;
           internal set;
    }
    public static string PropertyCompareMessage //#8
    {
            get;
            internal set;
    }
  public static bool MethodsMatching { get; set; }
  public static bool ClassnamesMatching { get; set; }

private static List<Dictionary<string,object>> getProperties(IEnumerable<ClassDeclarationSy
ntax> classes)
{
    return classes.SelectMany(c =>

        c.Members.OfType<PropertyDeclarationSyntax>()
                        .Select(pds =>
        new Dictionary<string, object> //C# 6.0 Feature
      //{ Dictionary Initializer saved the day }
{

//Class name where the property belongs
["ClassName"] = c.Identifier.ValueText,
["PropertyName"] = pds.Identifier.ValueText,
//The data type of the property
["PropertyDataType"] = pds.Type.ToFullString(),
//Attributes of the property
["Attributes"] = pds.AttributeLists
                   .Select(t => t.Attributes.ToFullString())
                   .ToList(),
//Whether the property is read only or not
["ReadOnly"] = pds.DescendantNodesAndTokens()
       .All(p => !p.Kind().Equals(SyntaxKind.SetKeyword)),
//Access modifiers of the property
["Modifiers"] = pds.Modifiers.Select(m => m.ValueText)
                   .ToList(),
//The body of the set call of the property
 ["SetBody"] = pds.DescendantNodes()
                          .FirstOrDefault(p =>  p.Kind().Equals(SyntaxKind.
SetAccessorDeclaration))
        ?.GetText()
        ?.Container.CurrentText.Lines
        .Select(l => l.ToString())
        .Where(m => m.Trim().Length != 0)
        .ToList(),
//The body of the get call of the property
 ["GetBody"] = pds.DescendantNodes()
        .FirstOrDefault(p => p.Kind() == SyntaxKind.GetAccessorDeclaration)
```

```
        ?.GetText()
        ?.Container.CurrentText.Lines
        .Select(l => l.ToString())
        .Where(m => m.Trim().Length != 0)
        .ToList()
}).OrderBy(t => t["ClassName"]).ThenBy(t => t["PropertyName"])).ToList();
}
```

I understand that reading the preceding code may be quite tiring and hard to understand. Because it was difficult to format the code here, I posted the same code on gist at https://gist.github.com/sudipto8 0/7c77c4b3bc879bb961a6.

The following code checks whether two properties match up or not—the expandList is a helper function:

```
private static string expandList(List<string> list)
{
    if (list.Count == 0)
            return " empty";
    return list.Aggregate((a, b) => a + " " + b);
}
//Checks whether two property definitions match or not.
public static bool DoPropertiesMatch()
{
        //First things first. If classes itself don't match up //there is no point checking
if the properties match up
      //or not
       if (DoClassesMatch())
       {
           var props1 = getProperties(Classes1);
           var props2 = getProperties(Classes2);
           StringBuilder propCheckBuilder = new StringBuilder();
           for(int i = 0;i<props1.Count;i++)
           {
             var attributes1 = props1[i]["Attributes"]
                            as List<string>;
             var attributes2 = props2[i]["Attributes"]
                            as List<string>;
             var modifiers1 = props1[i]["Modifiers"]
                            as List<string>;
             var modifiers2 = props2[i]["Modifiers"]
                            as List<string>;
             var getBody1 = props1[i]["GetBody"]
                            as List<string>;
             var getBody2 = props2[i]["GetBody"]
                            as List<string>;
             var setBody1 = props1[i]["SetBody"]
                            as List<string>;
             var setBody2 = props2[i]["SetBody"]
                            as List<string>;
             var propDataType1 = rops1[i]["PropertyDataType"]
                                      .ToString();
```

```csharp
            var propDataType2 = props2[i]["PropertyDataType"]
                                    .ToString();
            var readOnly1 = props1[i]["ReadOnly"]
                                    .ToString();
            var readOnly2 = props2[i]["ReadOnly"]
                                    .ToString();
            if (!modifiers1.SequenceEqual(modifiers2))
            {
              //Another C# 6.0 feature {String interpolation}
              //Make sure that these lines are appended in a
              //single line
              propCheckBuilder
               .AppendLine($"Modifiers are not  matching for
                 parameter { props1[i]["PropertyName"]} of
                 class {props1[i]["ClassName"]}");
              propCheckBuilder
               .AppendLine($"Ver 1 modifiers were
               {expandList(modifiers1)} and Ver 2 modifiers are
               {expandList(modifiers2)}");
            }

if (!attributes1.SequenceEqual(attributes2))
{
        //Another C# 6.0 feature {String interpolation}
        propCheckBuilder.AppendLine($"Attributes are not matching for parameter { props1[i]
["PropertyName"]} of class {props1[i]["ClassName"]}");
        propCheckBuilder.AppendLine($"Ver 1 attributes were {expandList(attributes1)} and
Ver 2 attributes are {expandList(attributes2)}");
}
if(propDataType1 != propDataType2)
{
        propCheckBuilder.AppendLine($@"Data type of property {props1[i]["PropertyName"]}
of class {props1[i]["ClassName"]} has been changed from {props1[i]["PropertyDataType"]} to
{props2[i]["PropertyDataType"]}");
}
if(readOnly1!=readOnly2)
{
   if(readOnly1.ToString()=="False")
   {
        propCheckBuilder.AppendLine($@"property {props1[i]["PropertyName"]} of class
{props1[i]["ClassName"]}  has been changed from readonly to settable property");
   }
   if(readOnly1.ToString() == "True")
   {
    propCheckBuilder.AppendLine($@"property
    {props1[i]["PropertyName"]} of class
    {props1[i]["ClassName"]}  has been changed from settable to
    a readonly property");
   }
}
```

```
//I left the getbody and setbody for you to implement
}
PropertyCompareMessage = propCheckBuilder.ToString();
return propCheckBuilder.ToString().Trim().Length == 0;
}
return false;
}
```

Copy and paste the code from https://gist.github.com/sudipto80/de55c1a99b6479ea761b.

Anatomy of a Class

As you know, there are few properties that distinctly identify a class from its peers. A couple of these are the class name and the base class from which it inherits and the interfaces that it implements.

Figure 5-8 shows an example.

```
/// <summary>
/// This is some thing
/// </summary>
class SomeThing: IClonable, IDisposable, BaseImpl
{

}
/// <summary>
/// This is some other thing
/// </summary>
class AnotherThing: BaseImpl, ISerializable
{
}
```

Figure 5-8. *Two classes*

At the topmost level, ignoring all other child elements, to check whether two classes match or not, it is sufficient to check their name and the base classes and interfaces they inherit from and implement. The following code checks whether two classes match at the topmost level as described:

```
public static bool DoClassesMatch()
{
    Classes1 = Tree1.GetRoot()
                .DescendantNodes()
                .OfType<ClassDeclarationSyntax>();

    Classes2 = Tree2.GetRoot()
                .DescendantNodes()
                .OfType<ClassDeclarationSyntax>();

//Checking whether classes from both code branches match or not
bool classesMatch = Classes1.Select(c =>
                        c.Identifier.ValueText)
```

```
                        .All(c => Classes2
                    .Select(cl => cl.Identifier.ValueText)
                      .Contains(c));

//Base list from all classes in version 1
var bl1 = Classes1.Select(c => new { ClassName = c.Identifier.ValueText, BaseList =
c.BaseList?.Types.Select(t => t.Type.ToString()).ToList() })
.ToDictionary( t => t.ClassName) ;

//Base list from all classes in version 2
var bl2 = Classes2.Select(c => new { ClassName = c.Identifier.ValueText, BaseList =
c.BaseList?.Types.Select(t => t.Type.ToString()).ToList() })
.ToDictionary(t => t.ClassName);

bool baseListMatch = true;

foreach(string key in bl1.Keys)
{
  if(bl1[key].BaseList == null | bl2[key].BaseList == null)
  //exlcusive or
  {
    baseListMatch = false;
    break;
  }
  if (!bl1[key].BaseList
     .OrderBy(t => t)
     .SequenceEqual(bl2[key].BaseList.OrderBy(m => m)))
  {
    baseListMatch = false;
    break;
  }
}

return classesMatch && baseListMatch;

}
```

The preceding code produces the output shown in Figure 5-9 when run with the following code snippets code1 and code2 as pasted in the gist:

```
https://gist.github.com/sudipto80/e21b7d4aaeabcbfe00e6

SmartComparer.Code1 = code_1;
SmartComparer.Code2 = code_2;
bool classesMatch = SmartComparer.DoClassesMatch();
bool propMatch = SmartComparer.DoPropertiesMatch();
bool methodMatch = SmartComparer.DoMethodsMatch();
bool isMatching = classesMatch && propMatch && methodMatch;

if(!isMatching)
{
```

```
        Console.WriteLine(@"The following differences
                          were found:");
        string mes = SmartComparer.PropertyCompareMessage +  Environment.NewLine +
        SmartComparer.MethodCompareMessage;
        Console.WriteLine(mes);
}
```

```
The following differences were found:

Data type of property Age of class Employee has been changed
from int  to double
property Age of class Employee  has been changed from settable
to a readonly property
```

Figure 5-9. *Differenences of code found by smart diff*

This preceding code produces the result shown in Figure 5-9.

The entire source code is available from https://gist.github.com/sudipto80/
c6f527430b89f6db118b.

Line #1 to line #6 helps load the codes in a structured way for SmartDiff class to perform the comparison. The getProperties() method returns the details about properties of a set of classes found in the source code being scanned. Methods, classes, and properties are checked for similarity based on a set of predefined metadata. If something doesn't match, a humane description is added to appropriate message. Later consumers of this code can use it for extrapolating it.

Just to put things into perspective, I compared the same two code snippets in Beyond Compare, and the result is shown in Figure 5-10.

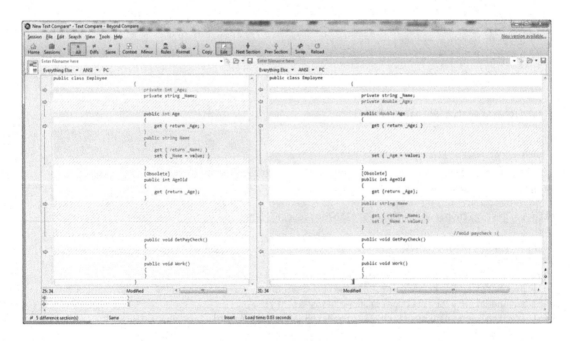

Figure 5-10. *Same code blocks compared in Beyond Compare*

As you can see, because of the order of property declaration, Beyond Compare is confused. That's fine because it's not a code comparer—it's a line-by-line comparer. But I think you got the gist of the idea of how Roslyn can help solve such issues. Do you see that it is possible to engineer an automerge tool using these code snippets that will work correctly almost always?

Detecting Plagarism

The simplest way to detect plagarized code is to check for a match in the token sequence stream.

Completely Duplicate Code

Identifying completely duplicate code is same as comparing the token stream obtained from both the sources.

Figure 5-11 shows code that generates a token stream for both of the examples code blocks and then compares them. You'll see that the token streams are identical, thus confirming a 100 percent match. Plagarized code that just differs in variables and functions or class names can be found using this scheme.

```
public double calcAvgSal(List<double> salaries)
{
    double sum = 0;

    for(int i = 0; i<salaries.Count ; i++)
        sum += salaries[i];

    return sum/salaries.Count;
}
```

```
public double calcAvgBonus(List<double> bonuses)
{
    double sum = 0;

    for(int i = 0; i<bonuses.Count ; i++)
        sum += bonuses[i];

    return sum/bonuses.Count;
}
```

Figure 5-11. *Possibly plagarized content*

Listing 5-2 finds probable duplicate code snippets by comparing token streams.

Listing 5-2. Finding Probable Plagiarized Content

```
string code1 =
@"public class PayRoll
{
        public double calcAvgSal(List<double> salaries)
        {
                double sum = 0;

                for(int i = 0; i<salaries.Count ; i++)
                    sum += salaries[i];

                return sum/salaries.Count;
        }
}";

string code2 =
@"public class BonusManager
{
        public double calcAvgBonus(List<double> bonuses)
        {
                double sum = 0;
```

```
            for(int i = 0; i<bonuses.Count ; i++)
              sum += bonuses[i];

            return sum/bonuses.Count;
        }
}";

var tree1 = CSharpSyntaxTree.ParseText(code1);
var tree2 = CSharpSyntaxTree.ParseText(code2);

var tokens1 = tree1
            .GetRoot()
            .DescendantTokens()
            .Select(t => t.Kind().ToString());

var tokens2 = tree2
            .GetRoot()
            .DescendantTokens()
            .Select(t => t.Kind().ToString());

tokens1.SequenceEqual(tokens2).Dump("100% Match");
```

The preceding code produces the output shown in Figure 5-12.

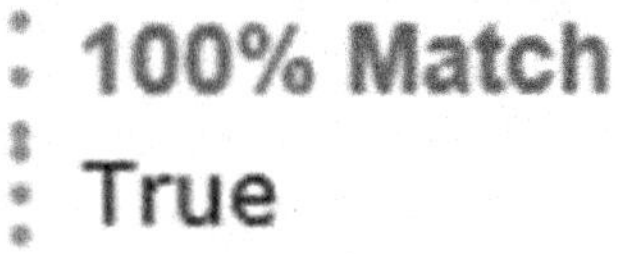

100% Match
True

Figure 5-12. *Result of 100 percent match*

The token streams are exactly the same, even though variable names are different. Figure 5-13 shows first few tokens and their values or names (in case of identifiers) for both code snippets.

▲ (20 items) ▶		▲ (20 items) ▶	
TokenType	NameOrValue	TokenType	NameOrValue
PublicKeyword	public	PublicKeyword	public
ClassKeyword	class	ClassKeyword	class
IdentifierToken	PayRoll	IdentifierToken	BonusManager
OpenBraceToken	{	OpenBraceToken	{
PublicKeyword	public	PublicKeyword	public
DoubleKeyword	double	DoubleKeyword	double
IdentifierToken	calcAvgSal	IdentifierToken	calcAvgBonus
OpenParenToken	(	OpenParenToken	(
IdentifierToken	List	IdentifierToken	List
LessThanToken	<	LessThanToken	<
DoubleKeyword	double	DoubleKeyword	double
GreaterThanToken	>	GreaterThanToken	>
IdentifierToken	salaries	IdentifierToken	bonuses
CloseParenToken	)	CloseParenToken	)
OpenBraceToken	{	OpenBraceToken	{
DoubleKeyword	double	DoubleKeyword	double
IdentifierToken	sum	IdentifierToken	sum
EqualsToken	=	EqualsToken	=
NumericLiteralToken	0	NumericLiteralToken	0
SemicolonToken	;	SemicolonToken	;

Figure 5-13. *First few tokens of two matching code snippets*

The boxed entries show where the names change, but the type of the token is the same. The following code generated the image shown in Figure 5-13:

```
tree1.GetRoot()
    .DescendantTokens()
    .Select(t => new { TokenType = t.Kind(),
                       NameOrValue = t.ValueText
                     })
    .Take(20)
    .Dump();
```

Just changing the variable to tree2 will get the tokens and their values or names for tree2.

Almost Duplicate Code

The challenge of identifying duplicate code becomes little bit harder when plagarizers go that extra mile and try to break functions apart like Figure 5-14 shows.

```
void fun()                              void fun()
{                                       {
        int x = 0;                              int y = 0;
        if(x<1)                                 doThose(y);
          dothat();                     }
        else                            void doThose(int y)
          doThis();                     {
}                                               if(y <1)
                                                    dothat();
                                                else
                                                    doThis();
                                        }
```

Figure 5-14. *Add new caption here*

As you can see, these code snippets are not exactly similar structurally, but they are doing the same thing. So, the way to attack this is to get a percentage score for the matching tokens. Listing 5-3 does that.

Listing 5-3. Finding Almost Similar Code by Percentage of Match

```
string code1 =
@"class A
{
        void doThat()
        {
        }
        void doThis()
        {
        }
        void fun()
        {
                if(x<1)
                        doThat();
                else
                        doThis();
        }

}";

string code2 =
@"class B
{
        void doThat()
        {
        }
        void doThis()
        {
        }
        void fun()
        {
```

```
                    int y = 0;
                    doThose(y);
            }
            void doThose(int y)
            {
                    if(y<1)
                            doThat();
                    else
                            doThis();
            }
}";

var tokens1 = CSharpSyntaxTree
                    .ParseText(code1)
                    .GetRoot()
.DescendantTokens()
                        .Select(d => d.Kind().ToString());

var tokens2 =  CSharpSyntaxTree
                    .ParseText(code2)
                        .GetRoot()
                    .DescendantTokens()
                .Select(d => d.Kind().ToString());

//Calculates the percentage of matching tokens.
Func<IEnumerable<string>, IEnumerable<string>, double> PercentMatch =
(tokenStream1, tokenStream2) =>
{
        int match = 0;
        for (int i = 0; i < tokenStream1.Count(); i++)
        {
                if (tokenStream1.ElementAt(i)
            == tokenStream2.ElementAt(i))
                        match++;
        }
        match *= 100;
        return ((float)match / (float)tokenStream1.Count());
};

PercentMatch.Invoke(tokens1,tokens2)
            .Dump("Percentage Match");
```

The preceding code produces the output shown in Figure 5-15.

Percentage Match
57.8947368421053

Figure 5-15. *Result of partial match*

This means that these code snippets match 58 percent roughly. However, you see that the doThose() method is code2 is almost the same as fun() method is code1. So if you apply this percentage match technique on pairs of methods, it will be even better.

Knowledge Mining

Today when software gets built by diverse teams with diverse skillsets in different locations, it becomes exponentially hard to pass the information to a new person joining the team. This is true irrespective of the experience of the person. Moreover, current tools (such as IDEs) are not capable of mining knowledge automatically from the source code, and thus developers lose the potential benefit of learning from each other. Roslyn can change all these. The following sections showcase several types of knowledge mining that can lead to a better understanding of the source code.

Design Pattern Mining

Identifying which design pattern is being used in a project is a subset of knowledge mining. The knowledge being mined is about the source code. It can be beneficial in many ways. First, it helps bridge the communication gap between veteran developers of the project and a newcomer.

It is almost impossible for a developer to scan through large codebases and identify patterns manually. But identifying these patterns can help newcomers in the project to better understand and visualize, and thus rationalize the architectural design choices made in the project.

In this section, you'll see how to use Roslyn to mine a few very frequent design patterns, like Singleton, Façade, and more.

Singleton Design Pattern Mining

Singleton is a popular design pattern (see Figure 5-16). Whenever developers want to make sure that there exists only a single copy of some object, they make that type as singleton. For example, connection objects, heavyweight objects (objects that are computationaly expensive to create) are generally created as Singletons.

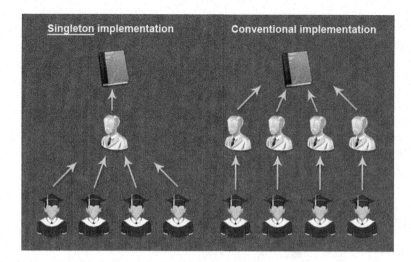

Figure 5-16. *Instances of Singleton classes*

When joining a new project, if experienced programmers are told that some of the classes are Singleton, they have a better idea about the design choices and rationale behind those. But in a large codebase, it may be impossible to figure out manually which classes are Singleton, unless the developer needs to instantiate one of such object. Listing 5-4 helps find Singleton classes from C# source using Roslyn.

Listing 5-4. Finding Singleton Classes from Source Code

```
var tree = CSharpSyntaxTree.ParseText(code);//#1
//Bottom up approach.
//Finding the return statements and then finding our path
//up till we find a class that seems to be a singleton.
var modifiers = new List<string>() { "public", "static" };

var staticFields =
tree
 .GetRoot()
 .DescendantNodes()
 .OfType<ClassDeclarationSyntax>()
 .Select(cds => new
{
        ClassName = cds.Identifier.ValueText,
        Fields =
        cds.Members
           .OfType<FieldDeclarationSyntax>()
           .Where(fds => modifiers.Any(mod =>
            fds.Modifiers.Select(m => m.Text).Contains(mod)))
              .SelectMany(fds => fds.Declaration.Variables
.Select(v => v.Identifier.
                                    ValueText.Trim())))

}).Dump("static fields");//#2
```

```
var staticReturns =
tree.GetRoot()
    .DescendantNodes()
    .OfType<ReturnStatementSyntax>()
    .Where(rss =>
      staticFields
        .SelectMany(f => f.Fields)
          .Any(f => rss.ChildNodes()
                          .Select(r => r.ToFullString())
                          .Contains(f)))
.Dump("static returns");//#3

staticReturns
.Select(r => new
{
//The name of the variable
VariableName = r.Expression.GetLastToken().Text,
//Type of the public method or public property
//that exposes the singleton instance
ParentType = r.Ancestors()

                .First(ty =>
                    ty.Kind()==
                                 SyntaxKind.PropertyDeclaration
                || ty.Kind()== SyntaxKind.MethodDeclaration)
                .ChildNodes()
                .First()
                .ToFullString(),

//Name of the class
//if the class is singleton, then this name and the ParentType
//Should match
Name = r?.
        Ancestors()?
        .OfType<ClassDeclarationSyntax>()
      .First().Identifier.ValueText
})//#4
.Where(r =>
//Checking whether the return type of the publicly
//exposed method or property match up the name of the class or //not
    r.ParentType.Trim() == r.Name.Trim()
//Checking whether the variable name used actually is of the //type being returned or not.
It may be possible for a class to //have many such functions
&& staticFields.Any(f => f.ClassName == r.Name
&& f.Fields.Contains(r.VariableName.Trim())))//#5
//Select just the names of the classes which seems to be //Singleton
.Select(r => r.Name)
//Dump those names.
.Dump("Probable Singleton Classes");
```

The line in the preceding code marked #1 loads the tree from the source code. Line #2 finds all the classes with at least one static field. Line #3 finds all the return statements that use at least one of the static field of any of the class. The projection at line #4 projects the type of the static field, the type of the public property, or the public method that exposes the static field and the type of the class that hosts the public property or the public method that exposes the static field. Line #5 filters elements from this projected list where the name of the class that hosts the public property or the public method and the type of the static field matches. These filtered elements are probably Singletons.

When run on the code at https://gist.github.com/sudipto80/790cb1aacf6b9b1e341d, it generates the output shown in Figure 5-17.

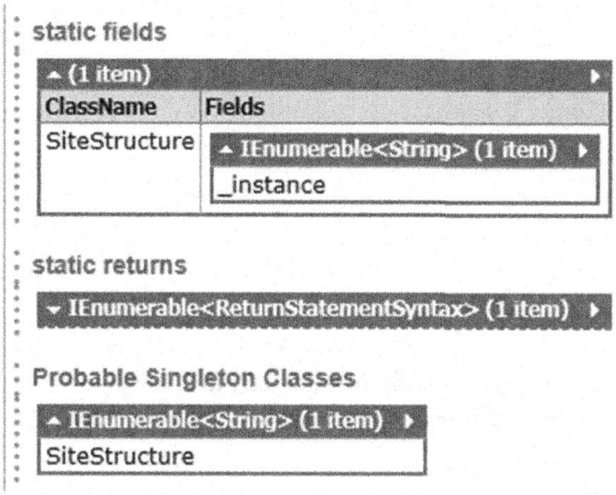

Figure 5-17. *Probable Singleton classes*

When run on the code at https://gist.github.com/sudipto80/7d65399d6b59ed488df8, the output generated is shown in Figure 5-18.

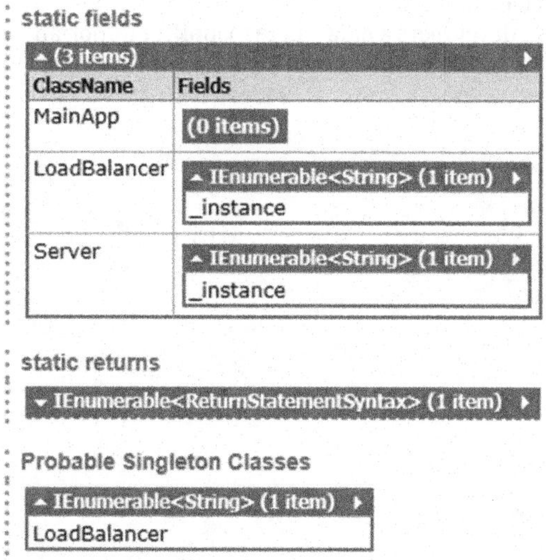

Figure 5-18. *Probable instances of Singleton classes*

111

When run on the code at `https://gist.github.com/sudipto80/21acbd428df4b3ba0619`, it produces the output shown in Figure 5-19.

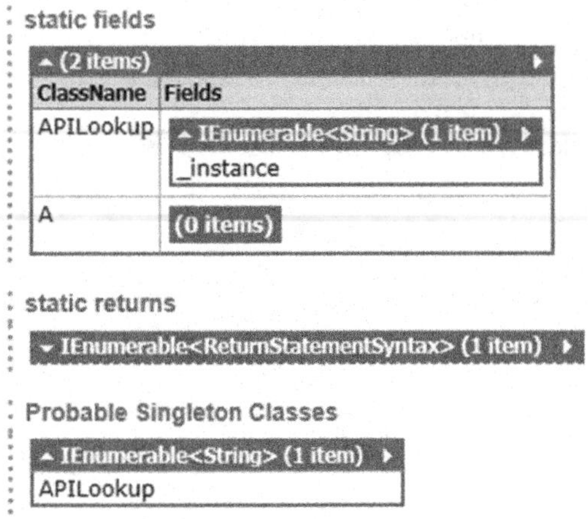

Figure 5-19. *Probable instances of Singleton classes*

I urge you to download the files from gist, run the script yourself with those, and try to tinker around with the script to see how it works. If you have doubts, plug in the magical `Dump()`method of LINQPad in between to see intermediate states of the data structures.

Façade Design Pattern Mining

Façade, as the name suggests, is the single point of contact for public client APIs to get many things done. For example, consider the classic example of a bank account. The bank account type may need many other types to get what the users of the bank account type wants, like capabilities to update account details, withdraw and deposit funds, and so on. For client code developers, the internal details of bank account type are not important, and they consider the bank account as a façade type.

Knowing which are Façade types in a big codebase gives developers a clue where to look for important functionalities. See Figure 5-20.

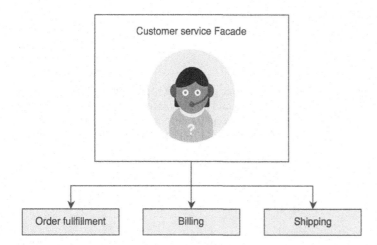

Figure 5-20. *Members of a sample façade class*

Listing 5-5 uses Roslyn to find out Façade types from a given code base. The assumption is that if a class has field of almost all other different types, then it might be a façade class/type.

Listing 5-5. Finding Probable Façade Classes

```
var tree = CSharpSyntaxTree.ParseText(code);

var classes =
tree.GetRoot()
        .DescendantNodes()
        .OfType<ClassDeclarationSyntax>();

var classNames = classes.Select(c => c.Identifier.ValueText);//#1

//classNames.Dump();
classes.Select(cds => new
{
        ClassName = cds.Identifier.ValueText,
 //Fields whose types are other classes/types declared before
 //and not pre-defined like int/float etc
 Fields = Convert.ToDouble
        (cds.Members.OfType<FieldDeclarationSyntax>()
.Count(fds => classNames
.Contains(fds.Declaration.Type.ToFullString().Trim()))),

//All the fields of the type
TotalFields = Convert.ToDouble(cds.Members.OfType<FieldDeclarationSyntax>()
.Count())

})//#2
//If almost all fields declared in a class are of known types //then the class might be a facade

.Where(cds => cds.TotalFields != 0
```

```
//75% of the all the declared classes are used
//as a field in this current class.
&& cds.Fields / cds.TotalFields >= 0.75)//#3
.Dump("Probable Facade Classes");
```

Line #1 finds the names of all the classeses declared in the source given. Line #2 projects the list consisting of the name of the class, total number of fields declared, in the class and number of fields of any other user defined type. The Where clause at line #3 filters out everything else except the suspected Façade types.

When run on the code at https://gist.github.com/sudipto80/c40146021017e7649d29, it produces the output shown in Figure 5-21.

Probable Facade Classes

▲ (1 item)		▶
ClassName	Fields	TotalFields
Mortgage	3	3

***Figure 5-21.** Probable Façade classes*

In this case, the Mortgage class uses all three predefined types, so it's a 100 percent match. In other cases, the script will report should there be a match of 75 percent or more.

Abstract Factory Pattern Mining

Abstract Factory is probably one of the most used design patterns. It's also quite complex to understand as many concrete and abstract implementations play a role in this pattern (see Figure 5-22).

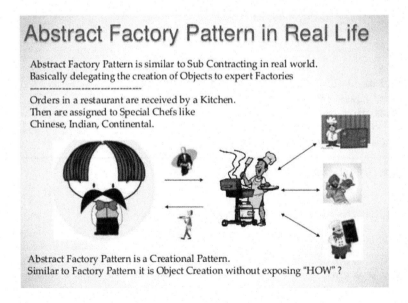

***Figure 5-22.** Usages of Abstract Factory pattern*

The UML diagram shown in Figure 5-23 represents the relationship between several participant classes in the Abstract Factory design pattern.

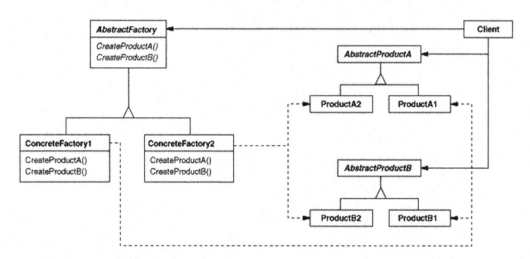

Figure 5-23. *Abstract Factory pattern in a UML diagram*

Listing 5-6 uses Roslyn to mine Abstract Factory patterns in source code.

Listing 5-6. Finding Probable Abstract Factory Instances

```
string code  = File.ReadAllText(@"code.cs");
var tree = CSharpSyntaxTree.ParseText(code);

//"ConcreteCreatorA" class overrides abstract method //"FactoryMethod" of abstract class
"Creator"
var abstractClasses = tree.GetRoot()
        .DescendantNodes()
        .OfType<ClassDeclarationSyntax>()
        .Where(cds => cds.Modifiers
          .Select(m => m.Text).Contains("abstract"))//#1
        .Select(cds => new
        {
                ClassName = cds.Identifier.ValueText,
                AbstractMethods = cds.Members
                  .OfType<MethodDeclarationSyntax>()
                        .Where(mds => mds.Modifiers
.Select(m => m.Text)                                              .Contains("abstract"))
                        .Select(mds => mds.Identifier.ValueText)
        })//#2
        .Dump("Abstract classes and Methods");

var relations =
        tree.GetRoot()
                .DescendantNodes()
                .OfType<ClassDeclarationSyntax>()
```

115

```
                    .Select(cds => new //#3
                    {
                            ClassName = cds.Identifier.ValueText,
                            OverriddenMethods = cds.Members
                        .OfType<MethodDeclarationSyntax>()
                            .Where(mds => mds.Modifiers
                                .Select(m => m.Text)
                                        .Contains("override") &&
                                        mds.Modifiers
                    .Select(m => m.Text).Contains("public"))
        .Select(mds =>
        new
        {
ReturnType = mds.ReturnType.ToFullString(), Name = mds.Identifier.ValueText
        }),//#4
        //Elvis operator saved the day
        InheritedFrom = cds.BaseList?.Types
                        .Select(t => t.ToFullString())
        })//#5
 .Where
 (
   cds => cds.InheritedFrom?.Count() == 1
   && cds.OverriddenMethods?.Count() == 1
 )//#6
.Dump(@"Abstract Factory Pattern Detected with
        following settings");
```

Line #1 finds the abstract classes from the source code. Line #2 projects a list of such abstract classes along with the names of the abstract methods. Line #3 finds such abstract methods that are overridden in a child class, and lines #4 and #5 find those subclasses that implement (by overriding) an abstract method of an abstract class. These filtered entries are suspected to be Abstract Factory patterns.

When run on the code at https://gist.github.com/sudipto80/a5eeef5abf58d7e03728, it produces the output shown in Figure 5-24.

Abstract classes and Methods

▲ (3 items)	▶
ClassName	**AbstractMethods**
AbstractFactory	▲ IEnumerable<String> (2 items) ▶
	CreateProductA
	CreateProductB
AbstractProductA	(0 items)
AbstractProductB	▲ IEnumerable<String> (1 item) ▶
	Interact

Factory Design Pattern Detected with the following settings

▲ (2 items)			▶
ClassName	**OverriddenMethods**		**InheritedFrom**
ProductB1	▲ (1 item) ▶		▲ IEnumerable<String> (1 item) ▶
	ReturnType	**Name**	AbstractProductB
	void	Interact	
ProductB2	▲ (1 item) ▶		▲ IEnumerable<String> (1 item) ▶
	ReturnType	**Name**	AbstractProductB
	void	Interact	

Figure 5-24. *Probable Abstract Factory design pattern instances*

Composite Design Pattern Mining

Sometimes the whole and part of the whole can and should be represented as a single object. That's the Composite pattern. It makes reasoning about several operations easy. For example, look at the org chart in Figure 5-25. If the number of reportees has to be calculated for each employee, it has to be done recursively until we encounter people who have no reportee. In the Composite design pattern, this type of node is called a *leaf*.

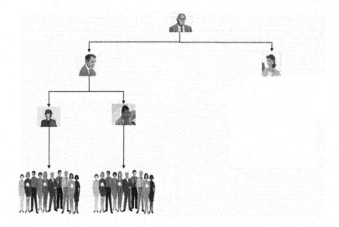

Figure 5-25. *Depiction of Composite design pattern*

117

Listing 5-7 finds occurences of Composite patterns in the given source code.

Listing 5-7. Finding Usages of Composite Pattern

```
string code = File.ReadAllText(@"composite.cs");
var tree = CSharpSyntaxTree.ParseText(code);
tree.GetRoot()
    .DescendantNodes()
        .OfType<ClassDeclarationSyntax>()
        .Select(cds => new
        {
                ClassName = cds.Identifier.ValueText,
                InheritsFrom = cds.BaseList?.Types
                .Select(t => t.ToFullString().Trim()),
                VariableTypes = cds.Members
                  .OfType<FieldDeclarationSyntax>()
                    .Select(fds => fds.Declaration.Type
                        .ToFullString().Trim())
        })//#1
.Where(
cds => cds.InheritsFrom?.Count() > 0
&& cds?.VariableTypes.Count() > 0)

.Where(
cds => cds.InheritsFrom.Any(b =>
        cds.VariableTypes.Any(v =>
//This assumes that the composite type will hold the leaf(s) in //a generic collection
        v.Contains("<" + b.Trim() + ">"))))//#2
        .Dump("Probable Composite Pattern Detected");
```

Line #1 creates a projection for all classes in the given source code, with three variables: the class name, the list of types it inherits from or implements (in case of interfaces), and the local variable declarations in the class. Line #2 filters only those that have at least one field declared that is a collection of any of the type it inherits from or implements. These classes are probably part of a Composite pattern implementation.

When run on the code at https://gist.github.com/sudipto80/11ad687c0aa4e0a01df8, it produces the output shown in Figure 5-26.

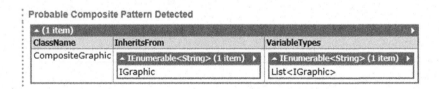

Figure 5-26. *Composite pattern usages*

Proxy Design Pattern Mining

Sometimes when developing applications, developers rely on the availability of some other services or programs. But those services or programs may remain unavailable for a long time. During this time, developers create a proxy of those services and return ideal values that they expect from those (see Figure 5-27). This is known as the Proxy design pattern. When the real object becomes available, the Proxy still shadows it. That gives developers the chance to test multiple implementations of the real object.

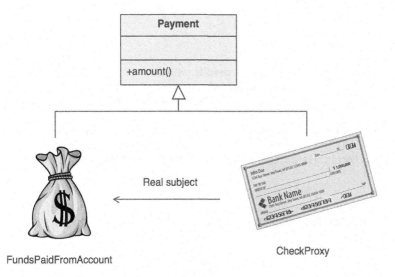

Figure 5-27. *Representation of Proxy object instances*

Listing 5-8 shows how to find out whether a set of classes represents a Proxy design pattern or not.

Listing 5-8. Finding Proxy Design Pattern Usages

```
string code = File.ReadAllText(@"proxy.cs");
var tree = CSharpSyntaxTree.ParseText(code);

tree.GetRoot()
    .DescendantNodes()
        .OfType<ClassDeclarationSyntax>()
        .Select(cds => new //#1
        {
        ClassName = cds.Identifier.ValueText,
        InheritedFrom = cds.BaseList?
                                .Types
                                .Select(t => t.ToFullString()
                                                    .Trim()),
        Fields = cds.Members.OfType<FieldDeclarationSyntax>()
.Select(fds => new
{
 TypeName = fds.Declaration.Type.ToFullString(),
 Variables = fds.Declaration.Variables
                .Select(v => v.Identifier.ValueText)}),
```

```
Invocations = cds.Members.OfType<MethodDeclarationSyntax>()
                        .Select(mds => mds.Body.ToFullString())
})//#2

.Where(
        cds => cds.ClassName!=null &&
        cds.InheritedFrom!=null &&
        cds.Fields!=null &&
        cds.Invocations!=null
        )//#3
        .Dump("Proxy Design Pattern Participants");
```

Line #1 creates a projection for all classes in the given source code, with three variables: the class name, the list of types it inherits from or implements (in case of interfaces), and the local variable declarations in the class. Line #2 creates different projections with the name of the filed, different methods, and the name of the host type.

Line #3 filters out elements that don't have any fields or have not inherited from any type. This leaves us with the probable Proxy types.

When run on the code at https://gist.github.com/sudipto80/8776d33d53750c6b6db4, it gives the result shown in Figure 5-28.

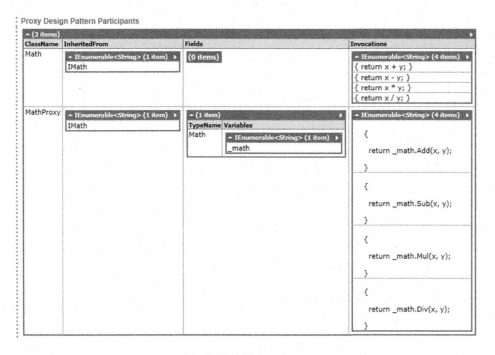

Figure 5-28. *Usages of Proxy design patterns*

As you can see, there are two classes, Math and MathProxy, both of which implement the IMath interface. However, Math is the real type, and MathProxy is the Proxy type—that's why MathProxy has a field of type Math. If you look at the invocations, it will be evident that MathProxy is the Proxy class.

Strategy Design Pattern Mining

The Strategy design pattern is commonly used to let the algorithm vary independently from clients that use it. It defines a family of algorithms, encapsurating each one and making them interchangeable, because they all implement a basic common interface, as illustrated in Figure 5-29.

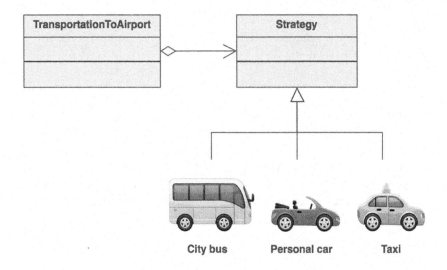

Figure 5-29. *Strategy design pattern example*

Listing 5-9 finds classes that are part of a Strategy pattern implementation.

Listing 5-9. Detecting Strategy Pattern Usages

```
//it scans only the given source. It doesn't search beyond the //given local file resource.
string code = File.ReadAllText(@"strategy.cs");

var tree = CSharpSyntaxTree.ParseText(code);

var abstractStrategy = tree.GetRoot()
            .DescendantNodes()
              .OfType<ClassDeclarationSyntax>()
              .Where(cds =>
          cds.Modifiers
            .Select(m => m.Text)
            .Contains("abstract"))//#1
              .Select(cds => //#2
          new
            {
                Name = cds.Identifier.ValueText,
                AbstractMethod = cds.Members
            .OfType<MethodDeclarationSyntax>()
```

```
                        .Where(mds => mds.Modifiers
                                 .Select(m => m.Text)
.Contains("abstract"))
                             .Select(mds => mds.Identifier.ValueText)
                        })
                    .Dump("Strategies");

tree.GetRoot()
    .DescendantNodes()
    .OfType<ClassDeclarationSyntax>()
    .Select(cds => //#3
     new
     {
     ClassName = cds.Identifier.ValueText,
     InheritedFrom =
                cds.BaseList
                   ?.Types
                     .Select(t => t.ToFullString().Trim()),
     OverriddenMethods = cds.Members
                     .OfType<MethodDeclarationSyntax>()
            .Where(mds => mds.Modifiers.Select(m => m.Text)
            .Contains("override"))
            .Select(mds => mds.Identifier.ValueText)
   })
.Where   //#4
(
  //Finds those classes that
  cds => cds.InheritedFrom?.Count() > 0).Where(cds => abstractStrategy
          .Any(s => cds.InheritedFrom.Contains(s.Name.Trim()))))
.Dump("Concrete Strategies");
```

When run on the code at https://gist.github.com/sudipto80/6678ab20e674e9612056, it produces the output shown in Figure 5-30.

Strategies

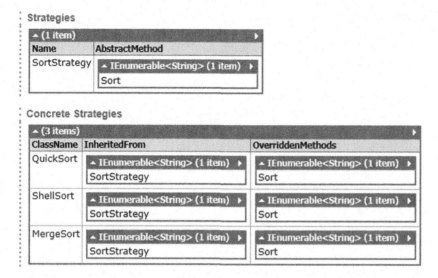

Figure 5-30. *Components of a Strategy pattern*

Line #1 finds all the abstract classes in the given source code. Line #2 lists all the abstract classes and the abstract methods. Line #3 projects the class name and the base classes/interfaces it inherits from or implements. Line #4 finds those classes that inherit from at least one of the abstract classes. These classes show probable usages of Strategy pattern.

Mining Frequent Nested Patterns in Code

Modern code Integrated Development Environments (IDEs) offer functionalities to insert common coding patterns that are required more often than others, like `try-catch` blocks, `if` blocks, and so on. These are pre-programmed into the IDEs.

That means IDEs are not programmed to take a note when new recurrent patterns appear in the source code. Ideally, programmers should never have to hand-create these patterns. They should be auto-curated by the IDE. Because the IDE sees all the code, it ideally sees more code than any individual developer.

The script in Figure 5-31 shows how nested patterns of varying depths (2 is the default) can be mined from given source code. Ideally, IDE should run a service in the background that looks for these patterns and auto-curate them, and developers should be able to search through these patterns and insert one if necessary. Moreover, because these patterns are language agnostic, that makes them even more interesting and useful.

Figure 5-31 shows some sample cases.

```
                                          foreach (..)
                     if (...)             {
if (...)             {                        foreach (...)
{                        if ()                {
    result = ...;        {                        try
    return result;       }                        {
}                    else                             foreach(...)
                     {                                   foreach(...)
if (...)                                              }
{                    }                            catch (...)
    result = ...;    if ()                        {
    return result;   {                            }
                         if ()                 }
}                        {                 }
if (...)                 }
{                    else
    result = ...;    {
    return result;
}                    }
if (...)             if ()
{                    {
    result = ...;    }
    return result;   else
}                    {
                     }
                     ...
                     }
                     continue;
                 }
```

Figure 5-31. *Showing some frequent nested patterns in code*

The first one shows ladder `if` blocks, the second one shows `if else` blocks, and the last one shows nested `foreach` statements.

Listing 5-10 finds such cases from source code given source code.

Listing 5-10. Finding Frequent Nested Patterns in Code

```
string code = File.ReadAllText(@"somecode.cs");

var tree = CSharpSyntaxTree.ParseText(code);//#1

var patternTokens = new List<SyntaxKind>()//#2
{
        SyntaxKind.IfKeyword,
        SyntaxKind.ElseKeyword,
        SyntaxKind.ForKeyword,
        SyntaxKind.ForEachKeyword,
        SyntaxKind.DoKeyword,
        SyntaxKind.WhileKeyword,
        SyntaxKind.TryKeyword,
        SyntaxKind.CatchKeyword,
        SyntaxKind.BreakKeyword,
      SyntaxKind.ContinueKeyword,
        SyntaxKind.OpenBraceToken,
        SyntaxKind.CloseBraceToken,
```

```
        SyntaxKind.SwitchKeyword,
        SyntaxKind.ReturnKeyword,
        SyntaxKind.ElementAccessExpression
};

//#3
Func<List<string>, int, List<IEnumerable<string>>>
toNgrams = (list, n) =>
{
        List<int> ints2 =
        Enumerable.Range(1, list.Count).ToList();
        List<IEnumerable<string>> breaks2 =
                        Enumerable.Range(0, ints2.Count / n + 1)
                        .ToList()
                        .Select(z => list.Skip(z * n).Take(n))
                        .Where(z => z.Count() > 0)
                        .ToList();
        return breaks2;
  };

var allPats = tree.GetRoot()
        .DescendantTokens()//#4
        .Where(t => patternTokens.Contains(t.Kind()))//#5
        .Select(t => t.ToFullString().Trim())//#6
        .Where(t => !t.Trim().Equals("{")
        && !t.Trim().Equals("}"))//#7
        .ToList();//#8

var dict =
toNgrams(allPats, 2)//#9
.ToLookup(t => t.Select(z => z.Trim())
        .Aggregate((a, b) => a + " " + b)) //#10
.ToDictionary(t => t.Key, t => t.ToList().Count());//#11

dict.OrderByDescending(d => d.Value)
    .Where(d => d.Value >= 2)
.Dump("Most frequent nested patterns");//#12
```

The first step in mining patterns from source code is to get rid of the redundant bits. Each pattern has a lot of metadata attached to it. For example, a for loop has a body and a range and a condition. These are all metadata for the for loop. While mining for frequent code path patterns, we should ignore this metadata as it will be different for a different instance of the same for loop pattern match.

In other words, patterns constitute of keywords. Take a look at the two examples in Figure 5-32.

```
int[] nums = new int[] { 1, 2, 4, 5, 214, 14}; int[] nums = new int[] { 1, 2, 4, 5, 214, 14};

for (int i = 0; i < 10; i++)              for (int i = 0; i < 10; i++)
{                                         {
    if (nums[i] % 2 == 0)                     if (nums[i] % 2 != 0)
    {                                         {
        Console.WriteLine(nums[i]);               Console.WriteLine(nums[i]);
    }                                         }
}                                         }
```

Figure 5-32. *Nested loops with similar patterns*

If you ignore the conditions, ranges, and so on, both of these have the same pattern, as shown in Figure 5-33.

```
for(...)
{
    if (...)
    {

    }
}
```

Figure 5-33. *Skeletal representation of nested pattern*

This skeletal representation of the frequent nested pattern can be written as for if in shorthand. So, given a nesting depth as an integer and a source code, these patterns can be extracted.

The code does that. In Listing 5-10, line #1 loads the source code to a syntax tree. Line #2 lists all the different keywords that need to be tracked to find the pattern. Line #3 creates a function that takes a stream of strings and generates a list of stream of strings representing the effect of moving a sliding window over the input stream. This function is used to generate several chunks of tokens, resulting in several streams of the given window size.

Line #4 all the tokens in the given source code. Line #5 filters only those that can possibly be used to make a pattern that is of interest. Line #6 projects these matching tokens' string representation. Lines #7 and #8 filter out brackets that mark the opening and closing of a block. Line #9 finds all the n-grams of size 2 from the given source code. In this case, the value 2 is the nesting depth. Line #10 creates a lookup table from this sequence where each key is a combination of two elements paired together. Line #11 creates a dictionary from this lookup table where keys remain the same, and values constitute of the matches. Line #12 filters elements for which there are less than two entries; because for all reasons it is safe to assume that unless a pattern occures more than two times, it is not worth to call it a pattern.

▲ IEnumerable<KeyValuePair<String,Int32>> (5 items) ▶	
Key	**Value ≡**
return return	138
if return	98
return if	84
else if	71
if else	67
	458

Figure 5-34. *Skeletal representations of some frequent nested patterns*

When run on the file at `https://gist.github.com/sudipto80/c27710fed74dbd99de60`, it generates the output shown in Figure 5-34.

Because `return return` can't be a valid pattern, we must ignore that. This is there because we got rid of the braces and thus function boundaries are removed. Moreover, `return if` can't be a valid pattern, but `if return` is. So, the way we must interpret this table is that `if return` and `return if` are the same. However, `else if` and `if else` are not because they are both valid patterns. This means that there are three prelevant patterns in this given file, as shown in Listing 5-11.

Listing 5-11. Showing Mined Patterns in Code

```
if (....) // Pattern #1
{
 return (...);
}

if ()// Pattern #2
{
}

else
{
}

else // Pattern #3
{
        if()
        {

        }
}
```

API Mining

Finding which methods of which types are more commonly used is important because it can help newcomers learn new important idioms on a priority basis and also can help identify important methods of the class. Moreover, this technique can also help identify the most vulnerable methods, the changing of which can cause a butterfly effect because those methods are used by a plethora of other components.

For example, a programmer who is new to network socket programming might not know where to start learning about it. The output of such an API mining script can help her. From this script it is evident that `TcpListener`, `TcpClient`, and `NetworkStream` are important classes, and most-used methods of these classes are also shown. This information can be used for self learning or for source planning of targeted training. Listing 5-XX finds frequently used methods.

Listing 5-12. Finds Frequently Used Methods of Several Types

```
string code = File.ReadAllText(@"code.cs");

var tree = CSharpSyntaxTree.ParseText(code);

var methodCalls = tree.GetRoot()
    .DescendantNodes()
    .OfType<InvocationExpressionSyntax>();//#1

var Mscorlib = MetadataReference.CreateFromFile(typeof(object)
                            .Assembly.Location);//#2
var System =  MetadataReference.CreateFromFile(typeof(System.Net.Sockets
                        .Socket).Assembly.Location);

var compilation =
        CSharpCompilation.Create("MyCompilation",
            syntaxTrees: new[] { tree },
            references: new[] { Mscorlib , System });//#3

var model = compilation.GetSemanticModel(tree);//#4

Dictionary<string,Dictionary<string,int>> methodCallMap = new Dictionary<string,
Dictionary<string, int>> ();//#5

foreach (var mc in methodCalls)
{
        var methodSymbol = model.GetSymbolInfo(mc);//#6
        string typeName = methodSymbol
                    .Symbol?.ContainingSymbol
                    ?.ContainingNamespace+
                      "." +
                    methodSymbol.Symbol
                    ?.ContainingSymbol?.Name; //#7
        string methodName = methodSymbol.Symbol?.Name;//#8

        if (typeName != null)//#9
        {
            if (!methodCallMap.ContainsKey(typeName))
            {
                methodCallMap.Add(typeName,
              new Dictionary<string, int>());
                methodCallMap[typeName].Add(methodName,1);
            }
            else
            {
                if (methodName != null)
                {
                        if (!methodCallMap[typeName]
```

```
            .ContainsKey(methodName))
                  methodCallMap[typeName]
        .Add(methodName, 1);
          else
                  methodCallMap[typeName]
          [methodName]++;
        }
      }
    }
}

methodCallMap
.Where(cm => cm.Key.StartsWith("System.Net.Sockets"))
.Dump("Call map");
```

Line #1 finds all the invocations of methods. Line #2 gets the assembly location of mscorlib.dll. Line #3 creates a compilation unit based on the given syntax trees and the mscorlib.dll location. This is an attempt to find out which methods are most commonly used. Line #4 creates an object of the semantic model. Later this model is used to ask some questions about the source code. Answers to these questions are important to finding methods and their base types when called. In line #5, a dictionary is created to store the number of times a method of a class is called. Next, the foreach loop iterates over all the invocations and gets the

Call map

▲ IEnumerable<KeyValuePair<String,Dictionary<String,Int32>>> (3 items) ▶	
Key	**Value**
System.Net.Sockets.TcpListener	▲ Dictionary<String,Int32> (3 items) ▶
	Key · **Value** ≡
	Start · 1
	AcceptTcpClient · 1
	Stop · 1
	3
System.Net.Sockets.TcpClient	▲ Dictionary<String,Int32> (2 items) ▶
	Key · **Value** ≡
	GetStream · 1
	Close · 1
	2
System.Net.Sockets.NetworkStream	▲ Dictionary<String,Int32> (3 items) ▶
	Key · **Value** ≡
	Read · 1
	Write · 1
	Flush · 1
	3

Figure 5-35. *Result of API mining*

method name (in lines #6 and #8), the Containing (the class which declares the method) class name (in line #7). Thise data is then added to the dictionary.

When run on the code at https://gist.github.com/sudipto80/d9f3eb0d68f96f3b37a8, the output shown in Figure 5-35 is generated.

Passing other assemblies as references other types and other methods can be found. Sometimes the programs can span upto multiple files. In those occasions several parsed syntax trees can be passed to the script, because a single parsed tree doesn't have information about other parsed trees. The semantic model is used.

Summary

In this chapter, you learned how Roslyn and LINQ can be used to extract several insights from your code that can be beneficial is many situations. For example, you found out how to find plagiarized code. In the next chapter you'll see how to use machine learning (ML) and Roslyn to find out with some confidence who the real author of a program is, because this question is very important when we know that plagiarism has happened and we must give credit to one of the conflicting parties. The techniques in the next chapter will help you determine who that will be.

CHAPTER 6

■ ■ ■

Code Forensics

In Chapter 5 you saw how to detect plagiarized code. This chapter is an extension to that. As I proposed in that chapter, imagine that two students submit code that looks plagiarized. Should credit be given for originality, and if so, who should get it? Who might be the original author and who might have been plagiarizing content?

The only way to know is to look at their submissions historically. The credit for originality should be given to the student whose code remains faithfully similar in patterns, historically. Techniques for determining this are collectively known as *source code forensics* or just *code forensics*. Using Roslyn and machine learning (ML) techniques, the original author can likely be found. Code forensics techniques rely on the fact that *habits die hard*. Let's say Tom is the original author and Mark copied from him. Mark has to try hard not to be detected by the plagiarism checker, whereas while Tom couldn't care less.

Every developer has a style. And if they don't try deliberately to hide their style like Mark, then that style will be evident and can be used as a digital signature or thumbprint to identify that developer uniquely from others.

Code forensics is generally used in legal matters where several parties claim to have authored a particular code. In this chapter you'll learn to develop a working algorithm for telling original authors and imposters apart. We'll put this algorithm to the test with some real code taken from other sources like GitHub.

To address this question, we first must understand how every developer differs in their style.

What Is Developer Style?

Each developer unknowingly and unavoidably develops a style as they grow in their career. Everybody has a different taste when it comes to naming variables and functions, for example. Level of knowledge of the programming language also plays a role. Some developers develop an affinity towards particular features, or particular data structures, and tend to use those more than other types of features or data structures. In general, looking at some code, a developer can tell whether she authored it or not.

Figure 6-1 shows a few example pieces of code written by a single developer taken from a blog.

© Sudipta Mukherjee 2016
S. Mukherjee, *Source Code Analytics With Roslyn and JavaScript Data Visualization*,
DOI 10.1007/978-1-4842-1925-6_6

```
public class C                          public class C                          public class C
{                                       {                                       {
    static void Main()                      static void Main()                      static void Main(string[] args)
    {                                       {                                       {
        C c = new C();                          C c = new C();                          dynamic d = 10;
        dynamic d = 10;                                                                 D del = d.Foo;
                                                c.M(z:Foo(), x:Bar(), y:Baz());      }
        c.Foo(d, 10);                       }                                       }
        d.Foo(10, 10);                      void M(int x, int y, int z) { ... }
    }                                   }
    public void Foo<T, S>(T x, S y)
}
```

Figure 6-1. *Some code written by a single person*

Note that this developer uses the identifier name Foo far too often. It's true that in computer programming literature, Foo and Bar are the two most abused words, but the point is that the developer is consistent in his choice of naming variables and methods. These three code snippets are taken from three different blog posts written by the same person. (If you are interested about the origin of foo and bar in programming literature, check out http://goo.gl/wfkaNH.)

Also note that most of the identifier names and method argument names given by the developer are *single character*. The developer is also familiar with *generics* and *dynamic* since such usages are found.

Extrapolating on these concepts, we can represent each programmer/developer as a *vector* (or *profile vector*) of several feature values. A *feature* in this context is nothing but a trait that is characteristic of a programmer. For example, a native English programmer will definitely use more diverse set of English words (in their full length) than their peer non-native speakers in variable and method names. Thus the percentage of valid English words used as tokens in variable names can be a feature. Some developers tend to use more inheritance than is arguably required. Some prefer long names, whereas some show a minimalist attitude when it comes to variable, method, and class names. These sorts of things often become second nature to the person. When plagiarizing content, developers may change the names of the variables, move methods, or refactor those into several classes or methods. But what they can't change (unless they try really hard) is their style—*that* is their very own.

Lots of things can be inferred from a developer's style. This chapter will use style to guess (automatically) who might have been the original author of a given program.

Elements of Style

Now that you have a fair understanding of what developer's style is, let's see how this style can be created from some features. The features in this section have been handpicked by yours truly as representative of the style a developer has.

MethodsPerClass

Some people write very few methods per class, try to represent even the smallest possible thing as a different class, and then write methods on those. These people are almost purist object-oriented programmers. They try to perceive every little thing as an object.

I'll try to explain the features that will be used and the rationale behind picking them. Mostly the choices made by developers are unconsciously driven by taste, culture, education, demographics and programming language knowledge.

ClassesPerNamespace

When people program in a team, it becomes harder to create a new namespace unless utterly required. Misplaced classes are found everywhere. Some developers get creative and create namespaces to arrange their classes, while some tend to put almost everything inside a namespace. A low number here can mean great taste as a developer.

PublicMethodsPerClass

Good object-oriented programmers know not to keep anything public unless absolutely required. However, some developers tend to keep more methods as public than are probably necessary. This can be a sign of less care for detail. We'll just use it as a number now in the profile vector.

PrivateMethodsPerClass

Most methods should be private by default. But some people tend to keep more methods private even if making them public would make a lot of sense. This is a sign that the person is feeling insecure about their code.

ProtectedMethodsPerClass

Not many people know how *protected* works. Very few people use it. So, just the existence of usage can be a potential clue to identify who is the author of a program.

OverriddenMethodsPerClass

People who uses inheritance more need to override their methods in the child types. A lot of overridden methods in a class mean that the class implements multiple interfaces and abstract classes. This is also a very important clue that is characteristic of the developer.

ParametersPerMethod

Sometimes developers are on a tight deadline and get little chance to refactor their code. Should a need occur to add an extra parameter to a method, they just add it. No blame. That's what most practicing programmers do. But some take the time to go back and change their code to make sure the parameter list remains manageable and easy to understand. Some developers pass in more parameters as loose variables, and some just wrap these parameters as an object and pass it along.

StaticClassesPerNamespace

Some people want to keep their classes as static. Some love extension methods, and extension methods can only stay in a static class in C#. That could be another reason. This number can mean that the person loves to extend things as required.

SealedClassesPerNamespace

Like *protected*, not many people know when *sealed* is appropriate. Although it means that the class can't be inherited, many programmers fail to see the point where it is absolutely needed. Not many programmers use sealed. Whosoever does use it can be tracked down easily.

PercentageOfMethodsWithVerbs

Any veteran programmer would give you the following tip about naming your variables: *Name your methods after verbs, because they do stuff for you. Name your classes after nouns, because they are things you want to use.* A high number in this field might mean that the programmer is experienced and knows his craft well.

PercentageOfEnglishWordsUsed

English is the language picked for naming variables, for the most part. Nobody is going to stop anyone from using the name of a variable taken from any other language. A large number of English word tokens used in variable, method, and class names could mean that the person is proficient in the English language, and the degree of diverse word tokens can help identify native English speaker programmers.

CodeToCommentRatio

Some programmers tend to be kind. They write great amount of comments to help the next set of developers (including themselves after a few months away from the codebase). Others (who think they are smarter than the rest of the planet) couldn't care less. That said, it doesn't mean good, kind programmers pour comments on their code—they write it based on their gut feeling. A low number here can mean that either the person is of the second kind or the code is really simple. A high number can mean that the code is really simple and probably self-documentary.

Vector Representation of Style

The idea is to represent these features in a vector (the profile vector of the developer). Figure 6-2 shows the representative form of how these vectors would look as a CSV row.

MethodsPerClass	ClassesPerNamespace	publicMethodsPerClass	privateMethodsPerClass	protectedMethodsPerClass	overrideMethodsPerClass	ParametersPerMethod	Tag
2.246153846	1.192307692	0.769230769	0.015384615	0	0.138461538	0.52739726	Toerlson
2.212121212	1.188679245	0.757575758	0.015151515	0	0.136363636	0.52739726	Toerlson
2.194029851	1.185185185	0.746268657	0.014925373	0	0.134328358	0.530612245	Toerlson
2.176470588	1.181818182	0.75	0.014705882	0	0.132352941	0.533783784	Toerlson
2.176470588	1.181818182	0.75	0.014705882	0	0.132352941	0.533783784	Toerlson
2.173913043	1.178571429	0.768115942	0.014492754	0	0.130434783	0.54	Toerlson
2.157142857	1.175438596	0.757142857	0.014285714	0	0.128571429	0.543046358	Toerlson
2.14084507	1.172413793	0.76056338	0.014084507	0	0.126760563	0.546052632	Toerlson

Figure 6-2. *First few rows of the profile vectors of* `Toerlson`

Each vector is generated from a source file authored by a developer—in this case, `Toerlson`. I have downloaded the source code for the book

Getting the Data for Experimentation

The program needed a lot of test data and there was a unique attribute required: The test data had to be programs written by a single individual. This meant that I couldn't download sources from a GitHub repository. So I decided to download source code for the following books, all published by Apress:

> *Pro C# 5.0 and the .NET 4.5 Framework* (by Andrew Toerlson) `www.apress.com/9781430242338?gtmf=b`

> *C# 6.0 and the .NET 4.6 Framework* (co-written by Andrew Toerlson Apress) `www.apress.com/9781484213339`

Introducing Visual C# 2010 (written by Adam Freeman) `www.apress.com/9781430231714`

Visual C# 2010 Recipes (co-written by Adam Freeman) `www.apress.com/9781430225256`

These books have lot of C# code, written by two prolific authors with different styles, and thus this looked like a perfect set of test data to feed my program. You can download these books' sources from each book's site.

You'll also need Humanizer. Humanizer is a .NET API for manipulating and displaying strings, enums, dates, times, timespans, numbers, and quantities in more human-friendly way. This project will be used to find out English words used by the developer. Download it from `https://github.com/Humanizr/Humanizer`.

Creating the Profile Vector

The vector representation shown in Figure 6-1 is the serialization of the profile vector for each programmer. The code in Listing 6-1 shows how to create a profile vector.

Listing 6-1. Creating Profile Vector Representation

```
public class Profile
{
        //Directory which stores code written by this author
        public string CodeDirectory { get; internal set; }

        //Representation of the profile
        //The keys represent the elements of style
        //and values represent the values calculated for each
        //code file
        private Dictionary<string, List<double>> Rows =
           new Dictionary<string, List<double>>();

        //All the source code syntax trees for all the sources
        //in the given directory.
        private List<SyntaxTree> CSharpForest =
           new List<SyntaxTree>();

        //Name of the author who's profile it is.
        public string Name { get; set; }
        public Profile(string name)
        {
            Name = name;
        }
    //Other methods to get the profile vector values
    //goes here.

}
```

Now create these methods for the Profile class:

```
private void PopulateRows(string name,int parts,int all)
{
   if (!Rows.ContainsKey(name))
      Rows.Add(name, new List<double>()
         { (double)parts / (double)all });
   else
         Rows[name].Add((double)parts / (double)all);
}
//Gets all the CSharp Syntax Trees in the given directory
public void GetTrees(int  n)
{
   foreach(var codeFile in Directory
               .GetFiles(CodeDirectory,"*.cs"
                  ,SearchOption.AllDirectories).Take(n))
   {
       try
       {
               CSharpForest.Add(CSharpSyntaxTree
               .ParseText(File.ReadAllText(codeFile)));
       }
       catch
       {
               //Nothing to do.
       }
   }
}
```

Finding MethodsPerClass

Add the method shown in Listing 6-2 in the Profile vector class to calculate the MethodsPerClass attribute.

Listing 6-2. Method for Finding MethodsPerClass Values

```
private void getMethodsPerClass()
{
   int totalClasses = 0;
   int totalMethods = 0;
   foreach (var tree in CSharpForest)
   {
       var classes = tree.GetRoot()
                       .DescendantNodes()
                       .OfType<ClassDeclarationSyntax>()
                       .ToList();
       totalClasses += classes.Count();
       totalMethods += classes.Select(t => t.Members
       .OfType<MethodDeclarationSyntax>().Count()).Sum();
       PopulateRows("MethodsPerClass", totalMethods,
       totalClasses);
   }
}
```

Finding ClassesPerNamespace

Add the method as in Listing 6-3 in the Profile vector class to calculate the ClassesPerNamespace attribute.

Listing 6-3. Method for Finding ClassesPerNamespace Values

```
private void getClassesPerNamespace()
{
    int totalNamespaces = 0;
    int totalClasses = 0;
    foreach (var tree in CSharpForest)
    {
        var namespaces =
          tree.GetRoot()
              .DescendantNodes()
              .OfType<NamespaceDeclarationSyntax>()
              .ToList();

        totalNamespaces += namespaces.Count();

        totalClasses += namespaces
         .Select(t => t.Members
         .OfType<ClassDeclarationSyntax>()
         .Count()).Sum();

        PopulateRows("ClassesPerNamespace",
        totalClasses, totalNamespaces);
    }
}
```

Finding Methods That Are of a Given Type

Add the method shown in Listing 6-4 in the Profile vector class to calculate the ClassesPerNamespace attribute.

Listing 6-4. Method for Specific Type of Methods Per Class

```
private void getMethodPerClassThatAre(string ofType = "public")
{
    int totalClasses = 0;
    int totalMethods = 0;
    foreach (var tree in CSharpForest)
    {
        var classes = tree.GetRoot()
                    .DescendantNodes()
                    .OfType<ClassDeclarationSyntax>()
                    .ToList();

        var methods = classes
                    .SelectMany(t => t.Members
                    .OfType<MethodDeclarationSyntax>()
                    .Where(z => z.Modifiers
```

```
                       .Any(dt => dt.ValueText
                       .Contains(ofType))))
                         .ToList();

              totalClasses += classes.Count;
              totalMethods += methods.Count;
    PopulateRows(ofType + "MethodsPerClass",
    totalMethods, totalClasses);
  }
}
```

Finding ParametersPerMethod

Add the method shown in Listing 6-5 in the `Profile` vector class to calculate the `ParametersPerMethod` attribute.

Listing 6-5. Method for Finding the `ParametersPerMethod` Values

```
private void getParametersPerMethod()
{
    int totalMethods = 0;
    int totalParameters = 0;
    foreach (var tree in CSharpForest)
    {
        var classes =
                tree.GetRoot()
                    .DescendantNodes()
                    .OfType<ClassDeclarationSyntax>()
                    .ToList();

        var methodsAndParams =

        classes
          .SelectMany(t => t.Members
          .OfType<MethodDeclarationSyntax>()
          .Select(z => z.ParameterList
          .Parameters.Count));

        totalMethods += methodsAndParams.Count();
        totalParameters += methodsAndParams.Sum();
        PopulateRows("ParametersPerMethod",
        totalParameters, totalMethods);
    }
}
```

Finding Sealed and Static Classes

Add the method shown in Listing 6-6 in the Profile vector class to calculate specific types (sealed, static) of classes in the code.

Listing 6-6. Method for Finding Specific Types of Classes

```
private void getClassesPerNamespaceThatAre(string ofType)
{
        int totalClasses = 0;
        var allNamespaces =
                CSharpForest
                .SelectMany(t => t.GetRoot()
                .DescendantNodes()
                .OfType<NamespaceDeclarationSyntax>()
                .Select(m => m.Name.ToFullString()
                  .Trim(new char[] { '\r', '\n', ' '
                    }))).Distinct()
                .ToList();
        foreach (var tree in CSharpForest)
        {
                totalClasses += tree.GetRoot()
                    .DescendantNodes()
                    .OfType<ClassDeclarationSyntax>()
                    .Count(t => t.Modifiers
                      .Any(z => z.ValueText
                            .Contains(ofType)));

                PopulateRows(ofType +  "ClassesPerNamespace",
                    totalClasses,allNamespaces.Count);
        }
}
```

Finding PercentageOfMethodsWithVerbs

Add the method shown in Listing 6-7 in the Profile vector class to calculate the ClassesPerNamespace attribute.

Listing 6-7. Finding PercentageOfMethodsWithVerbs

```
private void getUsageOfVerbsInMethodNames()//a high value here
{

  //got the list of verbs from here
  //http://www.talkenglish.com/vocabulary/top-1000-verbs.aspx

  //there are 1011 verbs in that list
  //for space constraint I have used only 5 here.
  //but you should use the entire list.
  string[] verbs = new string[]
  {"is","are","has","get","set" };
```

```
int methodsWithVerb = 0;
int allMethods = CSharpForest
        .SelectMany(t => t.GetRoot()
        .DescendantNodes()
        .OfType<MethodDeclarationSyntax>())
        .Count();

foreach (var tree in CSharpForest)
{
            methodsWithVerb +=  tree.GetRoot()
            .DescendantNodes()
            .OfType<MethodDeclarationSyntax>()
            .Select(t => t.Identifier.ValueText)
            .SelectMany(t => t.Humanize().Split(' ')
              .Select(z => z.ToLower().Trim()))
              .Distinct()
              .Count(z => verbs.Contains(z));

        PopulateRows("UsageOfVerbsInMethodNames",
            methodsWithVerb, allMethods);
}
}
```

Finding PercentageOfEnglishWordTokens

Add the method shown in Listing 6-8 in the Profile vector class to calculate the PercentageOfEnglishWordTokens attribute.

Listing 6-8. Finding PercentageOfEnglishWordTokens

```
private void getPercentageOfEnglishWordTokens()
{
  //A high value here can mean that the author is probably a
  //native English speaker
  var allWords = File.ReadAllText(@"t9.txt")
                    .Split(new char[] { '\r', '\n', ' ' },
                  StringSplitOptions.RemoveEmptyEntries);

  int allMethods = CSharpForest
                .SelectMany(t => t.GetRoot()
                .DescendantNodes()
                .OfType<MethodDeclarationSyntax>())
                .Count();

  int allNamesWithEnglishWords = 0;
  foreach (var tree in CSharpForest)
  {
        allNamesWithEnglishWords += tree.GetRoot()
                    .DescendantNodes()
                    .OfType<MethodDeclarationSyntax>()
                    .Select(t => t.Identifier.ValueText)
```

```
            .SelectMany(t =>
             t.Humanize().Split(' ')
             .Select(z => z.ToLower().Trim()))
            .Distinct()
            .Count(z => allWords
             .Contains(z.ToLower()));

    allNamesWithEnglishWords += tree.GetRoot()
            .DescendantNodes()
            .OfType<ClassDeclarationSyntax>()
            .Select(t => t.Identifier.ValueText)
            .SelectMany(t => t.Humanize().Split(' ')
            .Select(z => z.ToLower().Trim()))
            .Distinct()
            .Count(z => allWords
                 .Contains(z.ToLower()));

     allNamesWithEnglishWords += tree.GetRoot()
            .DescendantNodes()
            .OfType<PropertyDeclarationSyntax>()
            .Select(t => t.Identifier.ValueText)
            .SelectMany(t => t.Humanize()
             .Split(' ').Select(z =>
            z.ToLower().Trim()))
            .Distinct()
            .Count(z => allWords
             .Contains(z.ToLower()));

     allNamesWithEnglishWords += tree.GetRoot()
            .DescendantNodes()
            .OfType<FieldDeclarationSyntax>()
            .Select(t => t.Declaration.Variables
             .Select(z => z.Identifier.ValueText))
            .SelectMany(t => t.Humanize().Split(' ')
             .Select(z => z.ToLower().Trim()))
            .Distinct()
            .Count(z => allWords
                 .Contains(z.ToLower()));
    PopulateRows("PercentageOfEnglishWordTokens",
        allNamesWithEnglishWords,allMethods);
   }
}
```

Download the T9 dictionary from https://gist.github.com/sudipto80/2acccb95cd6d559bcf4c.

Finding CodeToCommentRatio

Add the method shown in Listing 6-9 in the Profile vector class to calculate the CodeToCommentRatio attribute.

Listing 6-9. Finding CodeToCommentRatio

```
private void getCodeToCommentRatio()
{
      int totalComments = 0;
      int totalCodeLines = 0;
      foreach (var tree in CSharpForest)
      {
         totalComments += tree.GetRoot().DescendantTrivia()
                  .Count(t => t.Kind() ==
                     SyntaxKind.MultiLineCommentTrivia
                  || t.Kind() ==
                     SyntaxKind.SingleLineCommentTrivia);
         totalCodeLines +=
                  tree.GetRoot().DescendantNodes().Count();
         PopulateRows("CodeToCommentRatio", totalComments,
               totalCodeLines);
      }
}
```

Generating CSV from the Profile

Normalized values for all the elements of style has been captured in a dictionary for each profile. The method shown in Listing 6-10 unwraps it (in other words, serializes the dictionary as a CSV file) where the headers represent the elements of style.

Because two or more profiles need to be dumped into the same CSV file before those can be processed further, the headers need to be dropped for all others. If includeHeaders is set to false (by default it's set to true), then only the values of the attributes (that is, elements of style) will be dumped.

Listing 6-10 shows how the profile vector is serialized to create a CSV out of it.

Listing 6-10. Method to Convert a Profile Vector to a CSV

```
public string ToCsvRows(bool includeHeaders = true)
{
      int count = CSharpForest.Count;
      List<string> rowsCreated = new List<string>();
      var headers =
        this.Rows.Select(t => t.Key).ToList();
      headers.Add("Tag");
      StringBuilder rowBuilder = new StringBuilder();
      if (includeHeaders)
        rowBuilder.AppendLine(headers.Aggregate((a, b)
                  => a + "," + b));

      for (int i = 0; i < count; i++)
      {
            List<string> cells = new List<string>();
```

```
        foreach (var h in headers
                    .Take(headers.Count - 1))
        {
            try
            {
                cells.Add(Rows[h][i].ToString());
            }
            catch
            {
                cells.Add("0");
            }
        }
        cells.Add(Name);
        if (cells.Count == headers.Count)
        {
            rowsCreated.Add(cells.Aggregate((a, b) =>
                    a + "," + b));
        }
    }
}

    return rowBuilder.ToString() + "\n" +
        rowsCreated.Aggregate((a,b) => a + "\n"  + b);
}
```

After this serialization to CSV, the profile vectors look something like what is shown in Figure 6-3. The headers are shrunk due to space constraints.

sealedCla	MethodsF	ClassesPe	publicMet	privateMe	protected	overrideN	Paramete	staticClas	UsageOfP	UsageOfV	AverageLe	CodeToCc	Percentag	Tag
0	4.5	1.076923	0.1875	0.0625	0	0	0.569444	0	0	0.128514	4	0.052821	0.506024	Troelson
0	0.987179	0.666667	0.217949	0	0	0.064103	1.207792	0	0	0.12	0	0.114871	2.04	Freeman
0	0.982143	0.666667	0.285714	0	0	0.089286	1.290909	0	0	0.11	0	0.118227	1.5	Freeman
0	0.986301	0.666667	0.232877	0	0	0.068493	1.222222	0	0	0.12	0	0.11878	1.94	Freeman
0	0.983607	0.666667	0.262295	0	0	0.081967	1.266667	0	0	0.11	0	0.119489	1.67	Freeman
0	0.933333	1	0.2	0	0	0.066667	1.178571	0	0	0.05	4	0.112526	0.81	Freeman
0.022727	1.915094	1.107527	0.811321	0.018868	0	0.132075	0.561576	0.045455	0.034483	0.506024	0	0.063437	2.160643	Troelson
0	4.785714	1.090909	0.214286	0.071429	0	0	0.492537	0	0	0.120482	8.75	0.051218	0.473896	Troelson
0	0.985507	0.666667	0.246377	0	0	0.072464	1.235294	0	0	0.12	0	0.11834	1.86	Freeman
0.022727	1.895833	1.1625	0.78125	0.010417	0	0.135417	0.565934	0.022727	0.034483	0.417671	0	0.062036	1.927711	Troelson
0	0.92	1	0.24	0	0	0.08	1.217391	0	0	0.05	8	0.123188	0.71	Freeman
0	0.983333	0.666667	0.266667	0	0	0.083333	1.271186	0	0	0.11	0	0.118955	1.63	Freeman

Figure 6-3. *Sample CSV representation of couple of profile vectors dumped together*

The values under the Tag column (Troelson and Freeman in this case) represent the names of the original author. You can find a sample CSV file at https://gist.github.com/sudipto80/a30056812fbc9baf20ed7e0270c96064.

We Have Profile Vectors—Now What?

Now that you have the data, you can use a supervised learning algorithm to predict who might have been the original author of a given source code. kNN (which stands for *k nearest neighbor*) is ideal for this situation. Because habits die hard and developers unknowingly leave traces of their habitual variable names and design choices in every source code file they create. kNN can take advantage of these facts. The next section briefly introduces the kNN algorithm.

kNN (k nearest neighbor)

In high school you learned about 2D point-based geometry, also known as coordinate geometry. Let's say we have two points in 2D space, as shown in Figure 6-4.

$$p(x_1, y_1) \text{ and } q(x_2, y_2)$$

Figure 6-4. *Coordinates of two points in 2D space*

The Euclidean distance between these two points can be calculated by the formula shown in Figure 6-5.

$$\sqrt{(x_1 - x_2)^2 + (y_1 - y_2)^2}$$

Figure 6-5. *Euclidean distance formula in 2D*

If you extrapolate this formula to *n* dimensions, it can be represented as shown in Figure 6-6.

$$d(\mathbf{p}, \mathbf{q}) = d(\mathbf{q}, \mathbf{p}) = \sqrt{(q_1 - p_1)^2 + (q_2 - p_2)^2 + \cdots + (q_n - p_n)^2}$$

$$= \sqrt{\sum_{i=1}^{n} (q_i - p_i)^2}.$$

Figure 6-6. *Generic Euclidean distance formula for n dimensions*

The idea behind using kNN as a classification algorithm is based on the fact that if two points are closer than others in an *n*-dimensional space, then probably those two points represents the same class—in other words, they are probably of the same type. Consider the following Figure 6-7. Let's say we want to find out the type of the green circle at the center with the question mark on top. Because there are two red triangles near the green dot and only one blue square, chances are high that the green dot is probably of the type that is being represented by red triangle.

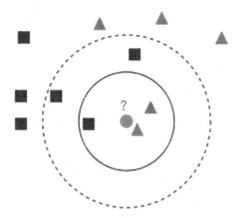

Figure 6-7. *Sample visual representation to perceive how kNN works*

Now you see that each row of the profile vector can be represented as a point in n-dimensional space, where n represents the number of elements of style we choose to use.

Once we have the representation of each code file as a CSV row as shown before, then we can sort points by their distance from the target point (target file) and then take first k points and count elements by each class. The class with the most votes wins.

Listing 6-11 implements a generic kNN capable of finding the distance between two points (in our case, two instances of CSV rows possibly representing two different author styles).

Listing 6-11. Generic Euclidian Distance Function

```
static Func<
            IEnumerable<double>,//The first vector
            IEnumerable<double>,//The second vector
            double  //Their Euclidean distance
         > Distance =
(fa, sa) => fa.Zip(sa, (a, b) => Math.Pow(a - b, 2.0))
            .Sum();
```

Listing 6-12 tries to guess the original author of a given document represented as a row of C# vector (or the CSV row).

Listing 6-12. Trying to Guess Who Might Be the Original Author

```
public static List<string> GuessWho(Profile author1,
                                    Profile author2,
                                    string testDataFile)
{
            string firstAuthorDetails = author1.ToCsvRows();
            StreamWriter sw = new StreamWriter(@"data.csv");
            sw.WriteLine(firstAuthorDetails);
            sw.Close();

            sw = new StreamWriter(@"data.csv", true);
            string secondAuthorDetails = author2
                    .ToCsvRows(includeHeaders: false);
```

```
            sw.WriteLine(secondAuthorDetails);
            sw.Close();
            //Index of the column named "Tag" is 14
            //So there are 13 features.
            //In supervised learning algorithm tag is also
            //called class and that's why the variable is named
            //as "indexOfClass"
            int indexOfClass = 14;

            var allInstances =
            File.ReadAllLines(@"data.csv")
                .Skip(1)//Skip header row
                .Where(l => l.Trim().Length > 0)
                .Select(f =>
                {
                        string[] vals = f.Split(',');
                        return new
                        {
                          Class = vals[indexOfClass],
                          Attributes = vals
                         .Where((v, i) => i != indexOfClass)
                         .Select(v => Convert.ToDouble(v))
                        };
                })
                .ToList();

    var allTestData = File.ReadAllLines(testDataFile)
                .Skip(1)
                .Where(z => z.Trim().Length != 0)
                .Select(t =>
                {
                    var toks = t.Split(',');
                    return toks.Take(toks.Length - 1)
                              .Select(z =>
                                  Convert.ToDouble(z))
                                  .ToList();
                }).ToList();

    List<string> guesses = new List<string>();
    foreach (var testData in allTestData)
    {
            guesses.Add(
              allInstances.Select(s => new
              {
                    Label = s.Class,
                    DistanceFromTestData =
                    Distance(s.Attributes,
                        testData.AsEnumerable())
              }).OrderBy(s => s.DistanceFromTestData)
              .Take(5)//k = 5
              .ToLookup(s => s.Label)
```

```
                .OrderByDescending(s => s.Count())
                .First()//The one with maximum voting
                .Key
        );
    }
    return guesses;
}
```

Demo on Troelson and Freeman's Code

Now that you have all the building blocks, you should be able to run a demo against the downloaded source code files. Listing 6-13 first creates the profile for the authors Troelson and Freeman and then gives a few sources that were originally authored by Freeman to check whether they system identifies the author or not.

Listing 6-13. Demo on Example Source Codes

```
//Creating profile for "Troelson"
Profile p1 = new Profile("Troelson");
p1.CodeDirectory = @"Pro C# 5.0 and the .NET 4.5 Framework_Andrew_Troelson_1";
p1.GetTrees(150);
p1.GetProfile();

//Creating profile for "Freeman"
Profile p2 = new Profile("Freeman");//adam freeman's profile
p2.CodeDirectory = @"Introducing Visual C# 2010_Adam_Freeman";
p2.GetTrees(150);
p2.GetProfile();

//Posing "Troelsons's" code as a unknown profile
Profile p3 = new Profile("Troelson");
P3.CodeDirectory = @"C# 6.0 and the .NET 4.6 Framework_Andrew_Troelson_2";
p3.GetTrees(15);
p3.GetProfile();

//Unknown profiles
Profile p4 = new Profile("Freeman");
p4.CodeDirectory = @"Introducing Visual C# 2010_Adam_Freeman";
p4.GetTrees(15);
p4.GetProfile();

//Create test data set
StreamWriter testDataWriter = new StreamWriter(@"testdata.txt");
//Some of the calculations involved might result in "NaN"
//and those are avoided by replacing with "0".
testDataWriter.WriteLine(p3.ToCsvRows()
                           .Replace("NaN","0"));
testDataWriter.WriteLine(p4.ToCsvRows(false)
                           .Replace("NaN", "0"));
testDataWriter.Close();
```

```
//Finding  the guesses
//who the system thinks is the author.
List<string> guesses = Profile.GuessWho(p1, p2,
                              @"testdata.txt");
```

Calculating Accuracy of the System

The following methods will help identify how good the system performs. In the demo, profiles of authors Troelson and Freeman had been disguised as unknown. However, since we know that these are their profiles, we can take advantage of that fact and check whether the guessed author matches the original author's name or not. If it does, the program was successful—otherwise, not. However, finding the percentage of time it was correct will be enough to check the performance of the forensics system.

Listing 6-14 returns the list of original authors from the test data.

Listing 6-14. Returning the Original Names of the Authors from Test Data

```
public static List<string>
GetOriginalAuthors(string testDataFile)
{
    return File.ReadAllLines(testDataFile)
                .Skip(1)
                .Where(z => z.Trim().Length != 0)
                .Select(z => z.Split(new char[] { ',' },
                StringSplitOptions.RemoveEmptyEntries)
                    .Last().Trim())
                .ToList();
}
```

Given the list of guessed names for authors and the original authors, the function in Listing 6-15 returns the percentage of time the results were correct. The higher this value, the better the program gets at recognizing programmers from their elements of style.

Listing 6-15. Calculates Accuracy of Code Forensics System

```
public static double PercentageCorrect
(List<string> guessedAuthors, List<string> originalAuthors)
{
    var correct = guessedAuthors.Zip(originalAuthors,
          (a, b) => a == b).Count(z => z == true);
    var all = guessedAuthors.Count;
    return (double)correct / (double)all;
}
```

Here I have used these following methods to calculate the percentage for this method, and the value I got was 0.8666666666666667. In other words, the program correctly identified the original author in 87 percent of times. Not bad, but with more careful feature selection this number can be boosted:

```
List<string> originals = Profile.GetOriginalAuthors(@"testdata.txt");
double correctness = Profile.PercentageCorrect
                        (guesses,originals);
```

Demo on GitHub Repositories

So far, you've seen how code forensics techniques can be used to identify single authors. In this section, you shall see how the same algorithm can be used to check whether a file is taken from a GitHub directory or not. For this example, I have used the source code of two very prominent projects on GitHub: CoreCLR and Roslyn itself.

You can get the source by clicking the Download ZIP button as shown in Figure 6-8. CoreCLR is available at `https://github.com/dotnet/coreclr`.

Figure 6-8. *Header of CoreCLR in GitHub*

Roslyn (Figure 6-9) is available at `https://github.com/dotnet/roslyn`.

Figure 6-9. *Header of Roslyn in GitHub*

Once you save the sources, write the code in Listing 6-16.

Listing 6-16. Using Code Forensics on Entire GitHub Repos

```
Profile coreclrProfile = new Profile("coreclr");
coreclrProfile.CodeDirectory = @"coreclr-master";
coreclrProfile.GetTrees(100);
coreclrProfile.GetProfile();

Profile roslynProfile = new Profile("roslyn");
roslynProfile.CodeDirectory = @"roslyn-master";
roslynProfile.GetTrees(100);
roslynProfile.GetProfile();
```

```
//Disguising coreclr profile as the unknown
testDataWriter = new StreamWriter(@"testdata.txt");testDataWriter.WriteLine(coreclrProfile.
ToCsvRows()
                .Replace("NaN", "0"));
testDataWriter.Close();

guesses = Profile.GuessWho(coreclrProfile, roslynProfile,
        @"C:\personal\testdata.txt");
originals = Profile.GetOriginalAuthors
            (@"C:\personal\testdata.txt");

correctness = Profile.PercentageCorrect(guesses, originals);
```

This time, correctness records a value of 0.99. In other words, this time the system was almost perfectly correct in identifying the GitHub repository from which the source was taken. However, you can see that this time, we applied the algorithm on the same (also called *training data*), unlike before when we used the algorithm on source codes that were previously unseen by the system.

Non-Obvious Usages of Code Forensics

Although the basic task of code forensics is to identify an original author from source code, there are several other ways we can put code forensics to good use.

Mentor-Mentee Association

In a good software development team, you'll always find people who are experts in their fields and people who want to be experts and are seeking mentors. Code forensics can help create the bridge between these two sets of people.

Suppose Mark wants to learn about the contextual keyword assembly, and we find that Troelson used the contextual keyword assembly 76.86 percent of times in his selection of all the contextual keywords (from the QuickWatch window shown in Figure 6-10). We can make the connection between Mark (mentee) and Troelson (mentor);

Name				"Troelson"
▲ 🔧 PercentageOfContextualKeyWords				Count = 8
▷ ▷ ● [0]		{[assembly, 76.8558951965066]}		Count = 142
▷ ▷ ● [1]		{[get, 11.4992721979622]}		Count = 14
▷ ● [2]		{[set, 10.1892285298399]}		0
▷ ● [3]		{[partial, 0.582241630276565]}		0
▷ ▷ ● [4]		{[yield, 0.436681222707424]}		Count = 39
▷ ▷ ● [5]		{[from, 0.145560407569141]}		null
▷ ▷ ● [6]		{[where, 0.145560407569141]}		
▷ ● [7]		{[select, 0.145560407569141]}		
▷ ● Raw View				

Figure 6-10. *Percentage of contentual keyword usages*

That is, if they work in the same team. Listing 6-17 finds the percentage of contextual keywords used in the source code by a given developer, and this can be a very important part of their profile.

Listing 6-17. Finding the Percentage of Contextual Keyword Usages

```csharp
private Dictionary<string, double> getPercentageOfContextualKeyWords()
{
    var  percentages = new Dictionary<string, int>();
    foreach (var tree in CSharpForest)
    {
       tree.GetRoot()
           .DescendantTokens()
           .Where(t => t.IsContextualKeyword())
           .Select(n => n.ToFullString())
           .ToLookup(t => t.Trim())
           .ToDictionary(t => t.Key, t => t.Count())
           .Where(z => !z.Key.Trim().StartsWith("//"))
           .ToList()
           .ForEach(t =>
           {
             if (!percentages.ContainsKey(t.Key))
                 percentages.Add(t.Key, t.Value);
             else
                 percentages[t.Key] += t.Value;
           });
    }

  return percentages
        .OrderByDescending(m => m.Value)
        .ToDictionary(t => t.Key, t => 100.0 * (double)t.Value
                    / (double)percentages
                 .Select(r => r.Value).Sum());
}
```

Newbie developers can also learn how to use data structures and classes from veterans. Listing 6-18 finds all the different kinds of data structures and classes used by a developer.

Listing 6-18. Finding All Different Kinds of Types/Data Structures a Developer Uses

```csharp
private List<string> getDifferentTypesOfObjectsUsed()
{
    var badChars = new char[] { '\r', '\n', '/' };
    return CSharpForest.
        SelectMany(t =>
      t.GetRoot()
        .DescendantNodes()
        .OfType<VariableDeclarationSyntax>()
        .Select(z => z.Type.ToFullString().Trim()))
      .Where(z => !badChars
        .Any(m => z.Contains(m))).Distinct().ToList();
}
```

When run on the the `Profile` class created earlier in this chapter, I got the list shown in Figure 6-11.

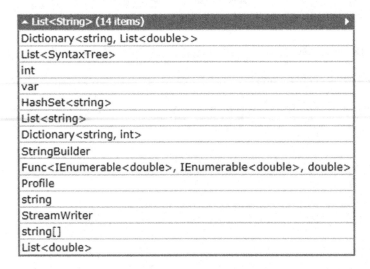

Figure 6-11. *Several data structures and classes used by a developer*

As you can see I have used `Func<>`, `Dictionary<>`, and `List<>` from the .NET core library. Thus, if anyone wants to learn about these data structures, then they can do so by me being a mentor if we (me and the person wanting to learn about these) worked in the same team.

This list can also be used to assign bugs. For example, if the author of a program gets to fix the bugs in their program, then they are likely to get the fix working faster than their colleagues. Looking at the preceding list, if some problem is reported on the class `Profile`, I'll be in a better position to fix that than any other person, because I created that class.

Such a service that calculates this data can be plugged in the source control repository pipeline to gather the data.

Data-Driven Developer Rotation

Developers often get bored in their current roles and wish they had something else to do. That something else more often than not is what their colleagues are doing for other parts of the project. For example, consider a developer who's been writing the so-called *middleware* for almost a year. She will definitely appreciate the opportunity to work for the public API layer or the data layer, where she would get the opportunity to learn the framework, expanding her horizon.

Developers who get many such opportunities get to use more keywords of the language and feel confident. There is a need to understand how diverse the area of opportunity presented to the developer is. Listing 6-19 calculates the percentage of keywords and contextual keywords used by a developer and returns the sum of these two numbers, which represents the spread of framework explored by the developer. The higher this number is, the more exposed the developer is.

Listing 6-19. Calculating a Numeric Value for Developer Familiarity with .NET Framework, Looking at Historic Examples Written by the Same Developer

```
public double GetDegreeOfCoverage()
{
    getPercentageOfKeyWords();
    getPercentageOfContextualKeyWords();
    var keywords = new string[] { "abstract", "as", "base",
        "bool", "break", "byte", "case",
        "catch", "char", "checked", "class", "const",
        "continue", "decimal", "default",
        "delegate", "do", "double", "else", "enum", "event",
        "explicit", "extern", "false",
        "finally", "fixed", "float", "for", "foreach",
        "goto", "if", "implicit", "in", "int",
        "interface", "internal", "is", "lock", "long",
        "namespace", "new", "null", "object", "operator",
        "out", "override", "params", "private", "protected",
        "public", "readonly", "ref", "return", "sbyte",
        "sealed", "short", "sizeof", "stackalloc", "static",
        "string", "struct", "switch", "this", "throw",
        "true", "try", "typeof", "uint", "ulong",
        "unchecked", "unsafe", "ushort", "using", "virtual",
        "void","volatile", "while" };

    var contextualKeywords = new string[] { "add",
     "assembly", "async", "await", "dynamic", "get",
      "global", "partial", "remove", "set", "value", "var",
     "where", "yield" };

int usedKeywords = PercentageOfKeyWords.Select(t => t.Key.Trim()).Count(z => keywords.
Contains(z));

int usedContextualKeywords =
    PercentageOfContextualKeyWords.Select(t =>
     t.Key.Trim()).Count(z => contextualKeywords.Contains(z));

return (double)usedKeywords / (double)keywords.Length +
                (double)usedContextualKeywords /
        (double)contextualKeywords.Length;
}
```

When run on the code samples from Adam Freeman and Andrew Troelson's books, I got the following results:

> For Troelson I got 1.1558441558441559.

> For Freeman I got 0.9935064935064936.

This means that Troelson has more exposure in the framework than Freeman. This finding is actually right. You can see that Freeman mostly wrote about ASP.NET, whereas Troelson wrote about the .NET framework. So if these two prolific authors were on the same team, you as a manager would know whom to rotate to a new position when asked for.

Summary

Code forensics is an active area of research, and as you saw in this chapter, it uses lot of machine learning. kNN is used in the chapter, but the accuracy can be improved if a neural network is fed the data. Currently, Deep Learning is becoming commonplace, so using those technologies also can yield a better result.

Elements of style should reflect the habits of the developer/programmer—something that developers/programmers can't change without trying real hard. A programmer who is inclined to choose Pascal case names will not choose camel case names, even when trying hard to avoid getting caught for plagiarizing.

In the next and final chapter, you'll see how all this number-crunching can be used to generate visually stunning, aesthetically pleasing visualizations that not only look good but also communicate the the state of health of your source code in a jiffy. As they say, a picture is worth a thousand words. See you there.

CHAPTER 7

Code Visualization

"Good coders code, and great ones steal." I read that quote somewhere. I have objections to the word *steal*. When people use something immensely great instead of writing their own, it's called *standing on the shoulder of giants*, and that's what I am set out to do in this chapter.

So far in the book you have seen how to use Roslyn and LINQ alongside C# to generate several meaningful metrics to determine code health. In this chapter you'll see how to glue these metrics with some stunning state-of-the-art visualization to be rendered in the browser.

You'll also develop some code to use the phenomenal visualization library D3.js. The motivation is that data collected from several metrices has to be represented in visually stunning, aesthetically pleasing visualizations. Another reason is that D3.js draws visualization based on transformation, so the same data (represented as JSON) can be used to generate several types of visualization. Let's say you have some data about how *dense* namespaces are, meaning how many classes are in them. Now you can represent this data as a D3 *treemap* or a D3 *circle packing graph*.

To use D3.js, we need to use some adapter code that will create a JSON representation of the metrices that we created in earlier chapters. The next section walks you through a D3.js script that draws a chart to show three major sections. Later you'll see how to put these together along with the results from the coding metrics.

Parts of a D3.js Script

Go to `https://d3js.org` and click the Examples link, as shown in Figure 7-1.

Overview   Examples   Documentation   Source

Figure 7-1. *The D3.js page header*

© Sudipta Mukherjee 2016

S. Mukherjee, *Source Code Analytics With Roslyn and JavaScript Data Visualization*,
DOI 10.1007/978-1-4842-1925-6_7

When the Example page renders, find the Bubble Chart icon as highlighted in Figure 7-2 and click it.

Figure 7-2. *Example page of the D3.js script*

Clicking the picture of bubble chart should take you to `http://bl.ocks.org/mbostock/4063269`. There you'll find the D3 script and the result. Scroll down to locate the boxed line shown in Figure 7-3.

index.html

```
<!DOCTYPE html>
<meta charset="utf-8">
<style>

text {
  font: 10px sans-serif;
}

</style>
<body>
<script src="//d3js.org/d3.v3.min.js"></script>
<script>

var diameter = 960,
    format = d3.format(",d"),
    color = d3.scale.category20c();
```

Figure 7-3. *D3.js script mention*

156

Scroll down little bit more to locate the data (Flare.json) on which this script operates to generate the bubble chart, as shown in Figure 7-4.

```
var bubble = d3.layout.pack()
    .sort(null)
    .size([diameter, diameter])
    .padding(1.5);

var svg = d3.select("body").append("svg")
    .attr("width", diameter)
    .attr("height", diameter)
    .attr("class", "bubble");

d3.json("flare.json", function(error, root) {
    if (error) throw error;
```

Figure 7-4. *Data loading of the D3 script*

If you scroll down further, you'll locate the Flare.json, file as shown partially in Figure 7-5.

flare.json

```
{
"name": "flare",
"children": [
 {
  "name": "analytics",
  "children": [
   {
    "name": "cluster",
    "children": [
     {"name": "AgglomerativeCluster", "size": 3938},
     {"name": "CommunityStructure", "size": 3812},
     {"name": "HierarchicalCluster", "size": 6714},
     {"name": "MergeEdge", "size": 743}
    ]
```

Figure 7-5. *Part of Flare.json file*

These are the three major parts of a D3 script:

- The D3.js script minified
- The data in JSON format on which the script will operate to draw the chart/ visualization
- The script itself (built inside the `<script>` tag in index.html)

Out of these three, we won't worry much about the first and last—we'll use them as is. To use D3, we need to convert our code metrics into JSON that D3 understands. In the next section, you'll create a bubble chart.

Creating a Bubble Chart

To get started, download D3.js minified from http://d3js.org/d3.v3.min.js and save it as d3.v3.min.js locally.

In this example, we'll create a bubble chart for the aspect ratio of method bodies. *Aspect ratio* is the ratio of the width and height of any rectangular box. If a line inside a method runs really long, then it becomes annoying, more so if the method is shorter. Thus a high aspect ratio is a bad thing for a method.

Finding the Aspect Ratio of Methods

In this example, we'll create a list of methods and their aspect ratio looking at a codebase.

The following list holds the details:

```
List<Tuple<string, string, string, double>> list = new List<Tuple<string, string, string,
double>>();
```

The first string is the filename where the class occurred, the second string is the name of the class, the third string represents the string name, and the last double represents that aspect ratio of the method.

The following code generates the aspect ratio of methods and puts the details in the list:

```
var codePath = @"D:\codeLocation";
foreach (var codeFile in
            Directory.GetFiles(codePath,
                "*.cs",SearchOption.AllDirectories))
{
  try
  {
      var code = File.ReadAllText(codeFile);
      var tree =
      CSharpSyntaxTree.ParseText(code);
      tree.GetRoot()
      .DescendantNodes()
      .OfType<MethodDeclarationSyntax>()                  .Select(mds =>
        new
        {
            ClassName = mds.Ancestors()
                          ?.OfType<ClassDeclarationSyntax>()
                          .First()
                          .Identifier.ValueText,
            MethodName = mds.Identifier.ValueText,

            Width = mds?.ToFullString()
                      .Split(new char[] { '\r', '\n' })
                      .Where(line =>
                      !line.Trim().StartsWith("//"))
                      .Select(x => x.Trim().Length)
                      .Max(), //#1
        Height = mds?.GetLocation()
                    .GetLineSpan().Span.End.Line -
            mds?.GetLocation().GetLineSpan()
                          .Span.Start.Line, //#2
})
```

```
.Select(mds => new
{
            ClassName = mds.ClassName,
            MethodName = mds.MethodName,
            Height = mds.Height,
            Width = mds.Width,
            AspectRatio = (double)mds.Width /
                        (double)mds.Height //#3
})
.ToList()
.ForEach(s =>
 list.Add(new Tuple<string, string, string, double>
 (codeFile, s.ClassName, s.MethodName, s.AspectRatio)));

}
catch { continue;}

}
```

In the preceding code, the line marked #1 finds the length of the maximum code line in the method body. That's the width of the method. Line #2 finds the height (which is same as the number of lines of the method) of the method. Line #3 uses a projection to use these two numbers to generate the aspect ratio of the methods.

Generating JSON from the List of Tuples

Now that we have the list of tuples, we need a way to convert this to a JSON that D3.js needs in order to plot the data, as shown in Flare.json file. The following method creates that. It uses some really involved LINQ queries that I'll explain.

As you saw, the JSON is hierarchical, so to represent that, the following data classes are needed. These classes are generated from the online utility http://json2csharp.com by copying some part of the Flare.Json file. The utility will generate the C# classes:

```
//Represents the Methodname and Aspect ratio relation
public class Child2
{
        public string name { get; set; }
        //size denotes the AspectRatio of the method
        public int size { get; set; }
}

public class Child //Represents the Class & Method relation
{
        public string name { get; set; }
        public List<Child2> children { get; set; }
}
```

```
//Represents the Filename & Class relation
public class RootObject
{
        public string name { get; set; }
        public List<Child> children { get; set; }
}
```

The following method generates the JSON that Bubble Chart needs. One fascinating fact you'll discover later is that the same data can be used by other D3.js charts. So this glue code (if you will) will be really handy:

```
public string ToBubbleChartJSON
(
   List<Tuple<string, string, string, double>> list,
        string name)
{
        List<RootObject> allNodes = new
        List<UserQuery.RootObject>();

        //Creating a dictionary to represent the
        //hierarchical structure of the JSON
        var dict =

      list
        .ToLookup(t => t.Item1)
        .ToDictionary(t =>
        t.Key.Substring(t.Key.LastIndexOf('\\') + 1),      t => t.Select(z => new      {

      ClassName = z.Item2,
              MethodName = z.Item3,
              AspectRatio = z.Item4
        })
      .ToLookup(m => m.ClassName)
      .ToDictionary(m => m.Key,
                                        m => m.Select(k =>

        new
        {
           MethodName = k.MethodName,
           AspectRatio = k.AspectRatio
        })));

        //Populating the list of RootObject
        //So that it can be serialized to generate the JSON
        foreach (var key in dict.Keys)
        {
                RootObject ro = new RootObject();
                ro.name = key;
                ro.children = new List<UserQuery.Child>();

                foreach (var ch in dict[key].Keys)
                {
                        Child d2 = new Child();
```

```
            d2.name = ch;
            d2.children = new List<UserQuery.Child2>();
        foreach (var zd in dict[key][ch])
        {
            Child2 s = new Child2();
            s.name = zd.MethodName;
            s.size = (int)zd.AspectRatio;
            d2.children.Add(s);
        }
        ro.children.Add(d2);
    }

    allNodes.Add(ro);
}

//Using Newtonsoft JSON.NET for performing the
// serialization
string json = JsonConvert
            .SerializeObject(allNodes,
        Newtonsoft.Json.Formatting.Indented);

return "{ \"name\":\"" + name + "\", \"children\":"
        + json + "}";
}
```

I know following the code there may be really difficult. So I have created a gist with the entire source code at https://gist.github.com/sudipto80/aee12f3ffa9123e4902d9100247eba42. You only need to provide the path of your source code, and it will work. If everything goes well, when executed in LINQPad, you'll see something similar to Figure 7-6.

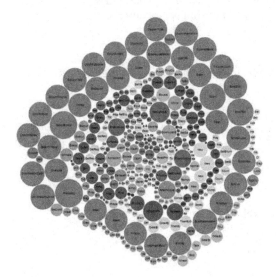

Figure 7-6. *Showing bubbles representing aspect ratios of several methods in a codebase*

The list has several categories: the filename, the method name, the class name, and the aspect ratio per method. The method *pivots* the list (or *unflattens* it, if you will) to generate a hierachial structure represented as a dictionary. This method converts the

```
List<Tuple<string,string,string,double>>
```

to

```
Dictionary<string,Dictionary<string,IEnumerable<>>>
```

where the first string in the dictionary represents the name of the file where this class and method is found. The key in the inner dictionary represents the class where the method is found. Finally, the value of the inner dictionary is an IEnumerable of anonymous types that hold the details of the method (method names and respective aspect ratio).

The loop (foreach loop) then iterates over this fabricated dictionary and generates a list of objects that represent the hierarchy. Finally, a well-recognized JSON API (Newtonsoft JSON.NET) is used to generate the JSON representation.

The code creates the data read by the script in index.html. To run the script, follow these steps:

1. Download index.html from D3.js site at `http://bl.ocks.org/mbostock/4063269`.

2. Download and save the D3.js minified version and save it in the same folder where you saved index.html in step 1.

3. Open index.html in your favorite editor and modify the line shown in Figure 7-3 to be like this:

   ```
   <script src="d3.v3.min.js"></script>
   ```

4. Download the script from the gist location and update the folders and file path as mentioned. Please read these comments and update the script before running it:

   ```
   //Provide your code directory
   string codeDirectory = string.Empty;
   //Make sure you have the D3.js minified version in the same //folder as Flare.
   json file
   //Provide your Flare.json file path
   string flareJSONFilePath = string.Empty;
   //Provide the path of your index.html file path
   //Make sure index.html resides in the same folder as //Flare.json and D3.js
   minified version
   string indexFilePath = string.Empty;
   ```

5. Now save the modified script (along with details about folders) in a folder and name it <whatever>.linq (don't forget the .linq extension).

6. Now point LINQPad to this file, and you're ready to run.

Re-using the Same Code for Other Types of Charts

Now that you can draw a bubble chart, let's look at how to use the same code with a changed script to make it a treemap. Figures 7-7 and 7-8 show the same data (Flare.json) represented in Treemap.

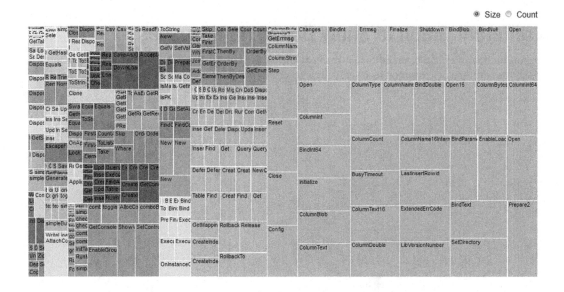

Figure 7-7. *Treemap by size*

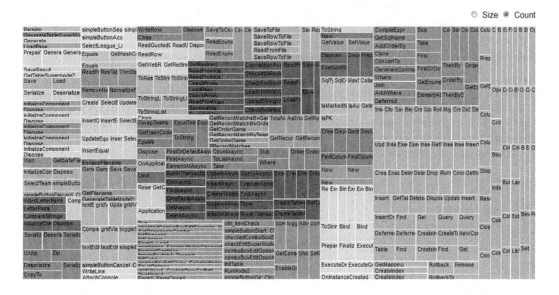

Figure 7-8. *Treemap by count*

You can see the fluid transition at www.youtube.com/watch?v=fIvmyPe2i4E. To use Treemap, you just need to change the index.html file as per the Treemap requirement, available at http://bl.ocks.org/mbostock/4063582. Note that Treemap and bubble charts both use the v3 version of D3.js.

If you want to use something else that relies on more current version of D3 (like v4), then make sure that the minified version of D3.js of v4 is made available locally. I know it may seem trivial, but that may be missed.

A Different Graph to Show Dense Namespaces

Running on Roslyn's main branch (Roslyn-master), the circle packing diagram in Figure 7-9 was generated. This shows several types wrapped in several circles representing their namespaces.

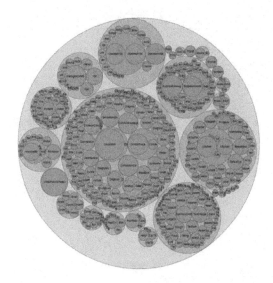

Figure 7-9. *Roslyn namespaces and types in circle packing*

You can see a demonstration of this visualization at www.youtube.com/watch?v=5s7Z7oNQfWo.

For this, the circle packing chart is used. You can download the index.html file for this D3.js script at http://bl.ocks.org/mbostock/4063530. But this chart relies on v4 of D3.js, so you have to download that and keep in the same folder.

The following code generated the data for this chart:

```
List<Tuple<string, string, int, int>> list = new List<Tuple<string, string, int, int>>();

foreach (var codeFile in
        Directory.GetFiles(@"D:\roslyn-master",
            "*.cs",SearchOption.AllDirectories))
{
    try
    {
        var code = File.ReadAllText(codeFile);
        var tree = CSharpSyntaxTree.ParseText(code);
            tree.GetRoot()
                .DescendantNodes()
```

```
                    .OfType<ClassDeclarationSyntax>()
                    .Select(cds =>
                            new
                    {
Namespace =
 cds.Ancestors()?.
OfType<NamespaceDeclarationSyntax>()
.First().Name.ToFullString(),
ClassName = cds.Identifier.ValueText,
MethodSize =
cds.Members.OfType<MethodDeclarationSyntax>()
.Count(),
ClassSize = cds.Members.Count
})

.ToList()
.ForEach(s => list.Add(new Tuple<string, string, int, int>(s.Namespace, s.ClassName,
s.MethodSize, s.ClassSize)));
}
catch { continue; }
```

This code is available at the following gist for you to follow along easily: https://gist.github.com/sudipto80/b677221e249ca6184179e1cc9e8ef509.

Summary

By learning how to draw bubble charts, treemaps, and circle packing, you found out how to use the fantastic D3.js framework examples to use for showing something really useful and neat. There are several different chart types that make sense to use for code visualization. For example, the Code Flower (www.redotheweb.com/CodeFlower/) or Coffee Flavor Wheel (www.jasondavies.com/coffee-wheel/) to represent dependency and inheritance relationships in a codebase, respectively.

I hope you have enjoyed this chapter and can now consider plugging in D3.js visualizations to your C# lists and dictionaries.

More boradly, I hope this book gave you a nice start and filled you with ideas on how you can use Roslyn and JavaScript visualization frameworks (like D3.js) to build code analytics systems for your team or company.

Index

© Sudipta Mukherjee 2016
S. Mukherjee, *Source Code Analytics With Roslyn and JavaScript Data Visualization*,
DOI 10.1007/978-1-4842-1925-6

Get the eBook for only $4.99!

Why limit yourself?

Now you can take the weightless companion with you wherever you go and access your content on your PC, phone, tablet, or reader.

Since you've purchased this print book, we are happy to offer you the eBook for just $4.99.

Convenient and fully searchable, the PDF version enables you to easily find and copy code—or perform examples by quickly toggling between instructions and applications.

To learn more, go to http://www.apress.com/us/shop/companion or contact support@apress.com.

Printed in the United States
By Bookmasters